Children,
Parents and Teachers
Enjoying Numeracy

Numeracy Hour Success
through Collaboration

3

3

Hamish Fraser
and Gareth Honeyford

David Fulton Publishers

This book is dedicated to Kate and Nina, without whom we would never have finished.

David Fulton Publishers Ltd
Ormond House, 26–27 Boswell Street, London WC1N 3JD

First published in Great Britain by David Fulton Publishers 2000

Note: The right of Hamish Fraser and Gareth Honeyford to be identified as the authors of this work has been asserted by them in accordance with the Copyright, Designs and Patents Act 1988.

Copyright © Hamish Fraser and Gareth Honeyford 2000

British Library Cataloguing in Publication Data
A catalogue record for this book is available from the British Library

ISBN 1–85346–639–5

Typeset by Kate Williams, Abergavenny
Printed in Great Britain by The Cromwell Press Ltd, Trowbridge, Wilts.

Contents

Acknowledgements

Books are never solely the work of the authors. People assist in many ways with writing and finishing. We will however avoid thanking everyone we have met for their help. The people that we acknowledge here have played important roles in the completion of this book.

A debt of gratitude is owed to the De Montfort University Maths Team, Peter Johnston-Wilder, Maggie Roddis and David and Irene Wooldridge; also to Liz Grugeon, another colleague at De Montfort University.

Primary teachers and others have given advice on chapters in this book. Julian and Nicky Milson and Linda Smiley have given particular assistance as have Sam Harris and Matt Quinn, the staff, parents and pupils of West Town School, Caspar Evans, Hugh Jones, Jaqui Lax, Martyn Honeyford and Ruby Bellamy.

We would also like to thank Dr A. R. Camina for his encouragement and Foreword.

We also appreciate the hours of proofreading provided by Margaret Camina, Nina Fraser and Kate Honeyford.

John Owens of David Fulton Publishers also offered crucial help with the book's publication.

Foreword

Dr A.R. Camina
Dean of Mathematics 1994–99, University of East Anglia

In 1494 Pacioli published his famous book on mathematics, *Summa de arithmetica geometria, proportioni et proportionalita*. He wrote this because he was concerned about the state of mathematics teaching in Italy at the time. Over 500 years later the government has published a National Numeracy Strategy for the UK. The need to understand the basic ideas of numbers, and consequently of mathematics, has grown over the past five centuries. We are constantly bombarded with information about 'inflation', 'interest rates' , 'mortgage payments' and 'APR'. Without public understanding it is easy for salesmen or politicians to mislead and confuse, either accidentally or deliberately. Even a statement like '90% fat free' gives an impression different from the equivalent '10% fat': a simple example of a number bond.

One of the themes of the National Numeracy Strategy is to encourage children to understand number bonds and to see their importance. This book explains how teachers can use the strategies to help children get to grips with these ideas. A strong feature is that it explains to parents how they can help their children positively. One of the difficulties with teaching mathematics is that many children, and adults, fail to grasp one particular concept and from then on the subject becomes a nightmare. This is called 'sum stress', and in Chapter 7 the authors discuss various ways of dealing with it. One might argue that this is the root of most problems connected with the teaching of mathematics.

As a professional mathematician it is a problem that I frequently encounter. On meeting someone for the first time people often ask what your job is. As soon as I say 'mathematician' there is normally a blank look on the face and they say that they could never understand it. They often expand and comment that it was OK until they had to do algebra, negative numbers or percentages. From the frequency of this response we can understand why it is respectable to say 'I cannot do mathematics'. Not being able to do mathematics is almost seen as a sign of the civilised person. If the National Numeracy Strategy is to work we need to create a new atmosphere about mathematics and numeracy.

The authors of this book explore many ideas and techniques for developing the National Numeracy Strategy into real situations in the classroom. One of the most important ideas to be introduced is that of 'Mental Maths'. This is not meant to be just 'mental arithmetic', which can be just rote-learning of tables, but is instead teaching children to think about sums and the way they do them. One of the great difficulties with rote-learning is that it is just as easy to learn something wrong, as right. One has only to listen to the performance of politicians and educators to realise how serious this problem is. Chapter 3 has lots of strategies to help the teacher and parent to use Mental Maths productively.

During a party I was approached twice by friends explaining to me that what had really confused them about mathematics was learning that 'a half multiplied by a half was a quarter'. This was surprising to me as there seemed to be little problem with this, but they went on to point out that 'multiply' means get 'bigger'; as in the Bible, 'go forth and multiply'. There were two surprising aspects of these conversations: they were entirely independent; and one was a native English speaker, the other a German speaker. The lessons we can draw from such anecdotal evidence are the importance of understanding ideas and what is meant by words like 'multiplying'. It also demonstrates the failure of rote-learning. The role of investigations in mathematics teaching is often controversial but is fundamental to trying to get a deeper understanding. It is, however, very demanding on teachers to make investigation work successfully. Chapter 6 contains many good ideas and ways of using investigations with children to deepen their understanding.

One of the earliest machines for counting was the hand and we still have recourse to our hands to do sums. This was common in Rome: Seneca wrote 'Greed was my teacher of arithmetic, I learned to make my fingers the servants of my desires'. In modern times we rely on the calculator or the computer. Consideration of how these modern devices can be used is the subject of Chapter 5. The authors make the important distinction between understanding computers and using computers – either as a tool for doing mathematics or as an aid for teaching. There is a popular belief that if there is a computer in every classroom the students will learn. This is a belief encouraged by the producers of both hardware and software. It is good to see these ideas examined critically and good advice given to parents and teachers to think carefully before buying software to aid children's education. This is not to say that software will not help, rather that it must be carefully evaluated.

This book is a welcome addition to the literature on mathematics for the young. The teaching of mathematics has a long history. Many attempts have been made to make it easy. Most have failed but we do make progress. In the seventeenth century an educator wrote that the mysteries of fractions were too deep for the average student to penetrate. Nobody would now believe that but we do have to keep trying to improve the teaching. This book and the way it makes the National Numeracy Strategy come alive will help to do this.

Preface

Once again, the very way that mathematics is taught is being challenged. The introduction of the National Numeracy Strategy, the continuing importance of Standard Assessment Tasks and the re-emphasis on 'going back to basics' all put pressure on teachers, parents and children. This book celebrates the good ideas and questions others. But most of all it is written for teachers and parents to promote the enjoyment of school mathematics.

Problems do exist in the teaching and learning of mathematics. Although traditional methods worked for many people, they did not work for all. They were based not on teaching children to think, but rather teaching them to follow a standard route to find the answer. Mathematics is often a stressful, upsetting experience for pupils, not always helped by teachers' own experiences. One teacher has recently reported a childhood experience when she 'trembled in front of a hushed class as she was humiliated by a sadistic teacher for failing to understand a mathematical problem' (Carvel 1999). This kind of experience is unlikely to produce good mathematics teachers, unless these negative experiences can be countered.

The National Numeracy Strategy is not a panacea that will solve all the problems of mathematics education. It will, however, provide an opportunity for schools to re-evaluate how they teach mathematics. With the National Numeracy Strategy arriving 'hot on the heels' of the National Literacy Strategy, it would be understandable if teachers were reluctant to adopt the ideas put forward in it. Its acceptance will also depend very much on how it is implemented. While it should provide teachers with an opportunity to review their mathematics teaching, it should not be forced upon teachers or seen as more change for the sake of change. Most importantly, it should be seen as a means of supporting pupils in developing numeracy. As French mathematician Didier Norman protests, mathematics teaching should be used not 'to stab young people through the heart' (Hannaford 1999), but rather as a tool for teaching children models of simple, complete, logical argument.

In this book we approach the subject from two perspectives: the theoretical background and the 'chalk-face' of the classroom. This reflects our current roles in education, academia and school. Throughout this book we refer to 'teachers'. This should be taken to mean not just professional teachers, but rather all adults involved with teaching children: parents, grandparents, youth workers, learning support assistants and so on.

Gareth Honeyford and Hamish Fraser
Peterborough, October 1999

CHAPTER 1

Background to the National Numeracy Strategy

The issue of enjoying mathematics will be discussed throughout this book. We believe that it is crucial that all parties concerned with developing children's mathematical skills should enjoy the process, but in this chapter it will emerge that enjoyment and mathematics are rarely identified together, and this issue must be addressed. This process can begin by considering the factors that affect the teaching of mathematics. The National Numeracy Strategy has a key role, but is not the complete solution. In this book we aim to extend expertise and confidence so that issues that make teachers less confident and less effective in their mathematics teaching are identified and eliminated.

The National Numeracy Project began in 1996 as a government funded research project to develop the teaching of mathematics. Within three years the National Numeracy Strategy emerged as the means to deliver the target of 75 per cent or more Year 6 children achieving level 4 or higher by 2002. Teachers are the agents through whom this goal can be achieved, so the success of the strategy rests with them and the support they receive.

Confidence, understanding and enjoyment

One of the issues facing many primary teachers charged with teaching mathematics is that they do not like mathematics as a subject and do not feel confident teaching it. This is not the case for every teacher but it is true for many. This lack of confidence in teaching mathematics can often be a key factor in reducing effectiveness and much of the pleasure to be had from teaching and learning mathematics. One London teacher provides the following example:

> I had been working for a few weeks in London's East End and, like most teachers early in their experience, I was nervous about my practice. I suspect that

there will always be subjects that teachers will feel ill equipped to teach. One of the issues and strengths, however, of the primary school system is that teachers are responsible for the whole curriculum. It is a burden that can at times be weighty. On this occasion, my worry focused on maths. As I walked through the large Victorian school, I passed the classroom of a teacher whose general competence I envied. She was bawling at the top of her voice. A child's understanding of place value had clearly distressed her. She exhibited a major shortcoming in personal, school and national practice: confusing getting the correct answer with evidence of understanding. She screamed, 'Just add a nought and don't worry about it'! This piece of advice speedily allowed the child to answer a range of set questions correctly and finally to escape to the playground. Was an understanding of place value established?

What is most striking is the transformation in this teacher. Clearly you would not envy the practice of somebody whose general demeanour was as described, but this was very out of character. Classrooms can be stressful, frustrating places and teachers can become very upset, but what this incident indicated was an additional stress above that of general classroom pressure. Crucially the point at which she felt least confident of her abilities as a teacher was when she taught mathematics. Equally significant was her frame of reference for teaching mathematics.

The teacher confided later that 'just adding a nought' had been how she was taught to cope with multiplication by 10. This is significant because it shows that her own experience of *learning* mathematics was her frame of reference for *teaching* mathematics. Other than their own experiences as pupils, teachers' points of reference have been limited to initial teacher training, teachers' resources, mathematics courses and in-service education and training (INSET). The National Numeracy Strategy is an opportunity to develop a significant point of reference.

Central to the work of the National Numeracy Strategy is mathematical understanding, and building connections between such understandings. This is important to teachers because the strategy provides a basis from which to locate teaching in developing children's understandings. We shall make a significant step if our focus becomes children's understanding and their feel for the number system, rather than the tricks that, with limited understanding, yield correct answers. Indeed, telling children to add a nought teaches them little of place value and is additionally dangerous because, although it works for whole numbers (e.g. $10 \times 23 = 230$), it is of no use with decimals: 10×2.3 does not equal 2.30. Teaching children to add a nought does not teach them that multiplying by 10 creates a number 10 times bigger. They need to know that when writing the new number each digit moves left one place past the decimal point. If there is no decimal then a nought is placed in the units column because the new number has no units. This is a central tenet of place value. It is this understanding that allows a fuller comprehension of decimals and percentages.

Once understanding becomes the goal of mathematics teaching, the ability to calculate effectively and fluently is improved. It is likely that children will still 'add noughts', but seeing the reason *why* this gives a correct answer is the foundation of subsequent understanding. The development of understanding will always be a higher objective than simply securing correct answers.

Research into primary teachers' understanding of key concepts in science and technology from the Scottish Council for Research in Education (SCRE) (1995) demonstrates that a third of the teachers in the study identified lack of background knowledge as a source of problems. Is this a factor with mathematics? Haylock and Cockburn (1989) identify weaknesses in the mathematical understanding of early years teachers; weaknesses that were diminished as the teachers confronted their shortcomings: 'The satisfaction expressed by teachers with whom we worked as previously-fuzzy ideas began to fall into place led us confidently to use the material from these discussions as the basis for this book' (Haylock and Cockburn 1989: x). Haylock and Cockburn also identify mathematical insecurity as common among student teachers. This lack of confidence is a complex issue, stemming from 'fuzzy ideas' or personal experience of mathematics, or both. The effect of these experiences is crucial and the National Numeracy Strategy will help tackle them for the benefit of teachers and pupils.

Mathematics in society

In many people's minds, mathematics is associated with negative feelings. On hearing a colleague mention his wider role in mathematics education during a computer in-service session, one course member declared, 'I'm no good at maths – I'm artistic'. This exemplifies what Haylock (1995) identifies as the social acceptability of being poor mathematically and, further, the belief that some people cannot be competent mathematically because of their gifts in other areas. This is supported by what the Office for Standards in Education (OFSTED) argues is our culture's readier acceptance of innumeracy than illiteracy (OFSTED 1997). The same publication also says that if children become anxious about mathematics because of confused or confusing teaching, attitudes to mathematics can become and remain negative, with destructive consequences for future achievement and enjoyment.

We have already examined, as one source of jumbled teaching, a teacher's own experience of being taught mathematics. However, this cycle could be significant for more than just teachers' attitudes. Surveys by Sewell (1981) and Cockcroft (1982) demonstrate widespread feelings of inadequacy and anxiety toward mathematics in the British adult population. These conclusions were subsequently confirmed by the work of Briggs and Crook (1991) and it seems evident that Britons generally lack confidence mathematically. This issue is present for most sectors of society. Buxton's

1981 study of negative emotions toward mathematics in 'articulate' and 'intelligent' adults demonstrated feelings of distaste, anxiety and incompetence in the face of mathematical problems. Strong negative feelings toward mathematics are prevalent in society and to change this situation for the better teachers need to break away from the negative experiences of their past. Failure to do so will perpetuate similar attitudes in pupils. The National Numeracy Strategy provides a basis from which to make this change.

The teaching of mathematics

Haylock (1995) gives an example showing how the intervention of a senior teacher damaged both the mathematical and social confidence of a young child:

> I remember when I was seven I had to do a hundred long divisions. The head-master came in to check on our progress. He picked me up and banged me up and down on my chair saying 'Why can't you do it?' After that I wouldn't ask if I couldn't understand something.
> (Haylock 1995: 4)

In examining this example several things are amiss. The task is clearly inappropriate for a seven-year-old; the quantity is disturbing; and the method (algorithm) needed to arrive at the correct answer is complex. Further, we have to assume that the head teacher was not in the classroom while the class worked. So we have difficult and inappropriate mathematics simply being used to occupy children. Is this likely to be an enjoyable experience? The damage this does to how mathematics is perceived is difficult to measure!

The National Numeracy Strategy and its structuring of mathematics will engage with such situations in a number of ways. Clearly it cannot deal with the gross professional misconduct demonstrated here, but it can address two matters that are wrong in the scenario. First, it places the responsibility on teachers to teach. When mathematics is taught, the teacher teaches it! Much of the strategy's structure emphasises this. Secondly, the strategy is explicit on the teaching of written algorithms. There is a great deal of evidence that their premature introduction is damaging to children's understanding. We will examine these issues in Chapter 4. Long division is a classic example of a written algorithm. Written methods or algorithms do not appear in any form in the National Numeracy Strategy until Year 3, and long division not until Year 6.

Teaching a subject that for some individuals has such unpleasant connotations will have an effect on a teacher's performance. This may make them more determined not to repeat errors they have experienced or it might mean that anxiety affects their own delivery of mathematics. An individual's subject confidence is central here.

Negative experiences need to be tackled. Teachers can often avoid teaching topics they don't enjoy. Some recent research we have been involved in examines confidence in handling data. Diffident teachers frequently do not teach this topic and probability is hardly ever tackled. When teaching mathematics with the National Numeracy Strategy, avoidance will be harder for teachers. Planning and teaching are structured around a termly plan, which is very prescriptive, ensuring coverage of the breadth of the National Curriculum each year.

A new understanding

Further, there is more to teaching mathematics effectively than knowing lots of mathematics. Here are three examples of mathematics teachers getting things wrong:

'There were few maths teachers who could grasp the idea of people not being mathematical.'

'The teacher just didn't understand why I had problems.'

'I always tried to avoid asking questions in maths lessons because you were made to feel so stupid if you got it wrong.'

(Haylock 1995: 4–5)

We need to appreciate that some people find mathematics difficult, understand the reasons behind this and deal with the problems sensitively (see Chapter 7). It is important to consider these experiences while reflecting on personal practice. Feelings of stupidity and isolation should not be acceptable in mathematics lessons. With the wider class discussion and interactive class teaching demanded by the National Numeracy Strategy, teachers must be even more determined to prevent pupils feeling like this. A confident teacher, with insight into the isolation which children can feel, is a powerful classroom practitioner. Understanding the feelings brought to mathematics lessons by some children is a first step in developing their confidence in mathematics.

Realising and appreciating the problems that some children have with mathematics is an asset in teaching it effectively. So too is reflecting on personal experiences of being taught mathematics and identifying why these were wanting. For good teaching the mathematical understanding of the teacher needs to be sound. This, however, is only one aspect of effective mathematics teaching. Fraser clearly thinks there are other important areas where expertise is required: 'Would our children's mathematics be improved by a greater understanding of maths by teachers at the higher end of the mathematical spectrum or by a deeper understanding of the stages of mathematical progress lower down?' (Fraser 1998: 22). A far-reaching mathematical ability, of itself, does not equip you to teach mathematics well to young and very young children. Clear mathematical understanding is only *one* of the forms of understanding needed to teach effectively. Fraser again makes this point: 'I have trouble seeing a skilled mathematician helping children in difficulty in Year 2' (Fraser 1998: 22). Subject knowledge is important, but the teachers' art is more than this.

A feeling of insecurity when it comes to mathematics is common and there are teachers whose mathematics will need further development. This statement may cause alarm and anxiety for some teachers. These feelings stem from personal insecurities about mathematics, which are a feature of our society. In this situation there are three important elements to consider:

- Teachers tend to belittle the mathematics they know. Identifying the areas that are sound and which specific areas to work on is crucial – and this process need not be a painful or lengthy one.
- Teachers tend to underestimate the amount of mathematics they know. It is likely that they know more mathematics than they expect to know. The opportunity of a personal review is useful to increase confidence. A confident teacher is a better teacher.
- The value of the National Numeracy Strategy in identifying clearly when areas of mathematics are to be taught and predicting when such areas will arise enables teachers to be prepared in advance.

Conclusion

It is clear that enjoyment and mathematics are not normally identified together, but there are clear reasons for ensuring that this essential aspect of raising mathematical achievement is developed. What is also clear is that for children to enjoy mathematics, teachers need to enjoy teaching it. The National Numeracy Strategy provides a basis to do this. In subsequent chapters we will explore issues affecting the implementation of the strategy. This book is useful in this process because it emphasises enjoyment of mathematics and critically tackles key issues in the strategy.

Change has been a constant in education for many years and this has had an effect on schools:

> The process by which teaching is changing and teachers are changed, I shall show is systemically ironic. Good intentions are persistently and infuriatingly turned on their heads . . . They threaten the very desire to teach itself. They take the heart out of teaching.
>
> (Hargreaves 1994: 3)

By developing the confidence of teachers, parents and children along productive paths, the teaching of mathematics and the achievement of children in conjunction with the National Numeracy Strategy can be significant. As Hargreaves indicates, however, some implementations do not always have the intended effect. If this happens to the National Numeracy Strategy, it will be a tragedy, as it represents a significant chance to change for the better the way mathematics is taught. This may put some heart back into teaching.

CHAPTER 2
What is Mental Maths?

Mental Maths is the process by which children, through discussion and practice, develop increasingly sophisticated strategies of mental calculation that are built on their increasing understanding of number. This understanding is further developed in Mental Maths sessions as strategies are explained and refined. In this chapter we explain why Mental Maths should be a feature of most mathematics lessons.

Mental Maths is a central component of the National Numeracy Strategy so there has been an increased awareness of it. We will examine why Mental Maths is such a productive tool for mathematical learning through two key issues. This is intended to be of use to all teachers and parents seeking to develop their own and, possibly, their colleagues' Mental Maths teaching and, so develop children's learning and enjoyment of mathematics. The issues to be explored are:

- how the Mental Maths of the National Numeracy Strategy differs from a 'traditional' understanding of mental arithmetic;
- how Mental Maths develops children's mathematical thought.

A health warning

The issue of jargon is evident in explanations of Mental Maths. The jargon often employs phrases like 'Children developing a picture of how numbers work' or 'Building a set of connections between numbers'. These phrases are accurate descriptions of what Mental Maths seeks to achieve but, like all jargon, they have the potential to hide meaning.

An experience of mental arithmetic

I have always been mathematically competent. This was particularly the case at primary school. One of my enduring memories is that being good at maths did not make it any more enjoyable. In fact in many ways it made things worse! Sometimes I wished that nobody knew that I had a talent for numbers. When I moved up to secondary school this would not be a mistake I would repeat. One reason for this is examined here.

Friday was maths day. The mornings were the usual diet of maths scheme work followed by a series of maths tests after play. Finally, the afternoon was taken up with graph drawing, though rarely data collection. Of this mathematical diet, the maths test was the most frightening. After play everyone was told to stand up. The teacher, who had the status of a numeracy goddess, would walk up and down asking questions. If you hesitated or gave a wrong answer you had to sit down. Some weeks this *hors d'oeuvre* would not take place. Playing this game of mathematical skittles was strangely frightening and occasionally exciting but always stressful. If you sat down early you were in trouble. This could be just ridicule or punishment. Even winning was no release because a win would be required again next week!

On reflection, those with the biggest disadvantage were the children who found mathematics difficult. As nothing was ever discussed, and no strategies ever explained in detail, the same children would generally sit down first and the same group would be the last. As a member of the good mathematics group my fear was that I'd make a mistake and join another group.

Reflection on childhood experience is always a difficult thing. My impression is that mathematics teaching like this was normal. Mathematics was abstract and obscure – many children didn't understand it and would always find it difficult. That we didn't enjoy it was accepted because mathematics was troublesome and rarely enjoyed. Our parents thought 'skittles' was an excellent idea. They saw it as effective teaching of times tables, one of the building blocks of mathematics. That it was not particularly effective further increased the difficulties of the least successful. Despite repeated practice and clear identification of problems they did not improve significantly.

After skittles we would go straight into the main course – a test. The test was particularly stressful and I found it especially unpleasant. It was conducted under exam conditions, talking was forbidden, and it was structured to identify what was not understood. This 'discovery' was frequently not a new one for many children. The test consisted of 30 mathematics questions read out by the teacher. These were predominantly multiplication and division with an odd pot-pourri of 'problems'. I found this situation the most stressful. After the teacher had called out the 30 questions, answers were collected and then redistributed for marking. Once the class had marked their peers' work they were passed out to their owners and the teacher called the register to enter this week's score. My fear was that I wouldn't get 30. My realisation now is that for all the stress these tests involved they taught very little, except that mathematics should be despised.

The limitations of Mental Maths structured in this way will become clearer when we examine the role of discussion. I have no doubt that in the vast majority of situations the teachers who taught my classmates and myself were following the good practice of the day and had the best interests of the class and children in the forefront of their minds. My father was educated until he was 15 in Glasgow during the Second World War. When I discuss his experience of school, I am grateful for mine. It is danger-ous and a little unfair to chastise the past for not being today, but it is important to learn from it.

Mental Maths

The importance of Mental Maths was identified in a variety of publications (e.g. Askew *et al.* 1997; Cockcroft 1982), and it has also been a part of the non-statutory guidance for mathematics in all versions of the National Curriculum, so it is not a new phenomenon. The National Numeracy Strategy is, however, the first attempt to integrate it systematically in schools. There is a clear distinction between the Mental Maths of the National Numeracy Strategy and the oral questioning and drilling of children in traditional mathematics procedures (see 'An experience of mental arith-metic'). As Welch (1889) wrote, mental calculation is important: 'Mental arithmetic should precede and accompany written arithmetic. Exercise in rapid calculation should be frequent. Exercises for drill in rapid calculation should be given almost daily' Welch (1889: 116).

Although the mental arithmetic described by Welch has something in common with the Mental Maths of the National Numeracy Strategy – frequent daily practice linked with written methods – it is not the same. Anne Corfield describes one of the differences between mental arithmetic and Mental Maths:

'Mental Mathematics (rather than mental *arithmetic*) involves children (and adults) in a network of ideas. It encourages them to develop strategies for solv-ing problems and helps them to develop an understanding of *number* rather than *numbers to which certain standard things have to be done in order to solve a problem*. [original emphasis]'

(Corfield 1999: 6)

The phrase 'network of ideas' could return us to the jargon that surrounds Mental Maths. What Corfield is referring to here is working on problems that draw on all the pupils' experiences of number. This statement is best supported with an example:

The children were dealt 5 digit cards and were asked to make the closest possible total to 100. The children were not told which arithmetical operation to use. They were asked to explain how they arrived at their answer and why they thought they could not get another closer to 100.   (Corfield 1999: 7)

In this example the class are asked to draw upon a wide range of mathematics and knowledge of numbers, and they are required to be inventive and imaginative. By working in this way they develop a whole understanding of mathematics, which is no longer fragmented by their use of it in a variety of contexts. Giving experience that draws upon different strands of mathematics to resolve challenging problems is a powerful tool in its teaching. It should also be an enjoyable process.

Mental Maths requires children to develop personal strategies that are far more than number facts and procedures committed to memory (drills). Much of the mental arithmetic previously used as part of mathematics teaching relied heavily on this pedagogy, but this is not a style of teaching that is particularly fruitful for developing understanding. Children will still learn number facts with the National Numeracy Strategy but their importance is linked to developing strategies. This has significant advantages over drills.

- Children will have different ways of obtaining an answer. Sharing these methods allows them to be refined (through discussion) and provides a forum of which all are a part. This forum can be very powerful in developing children's mathematical thinking.
- Discussions allow the identification of children's errors and misunderstandings and are a powerful tool for developing children's mathematical thinking.
- Discussion is also a forum for children to gain experience of using correct mathematical language.

Lessons to learn from rapid mental arithmetic

There is much to draw from Welch's (1889) understanding of rapid calculation and the experience of mental arithmetic described above. Discussion is crucial for the effective application of Mental Maths. Its absence in more traditional mathematics is a consequence of the emphasis on developing rote learning through testing rather than understanding. Using Mental Maths children should develop strategies of mental calculation in conjunction with understanding.

In test situations you are not allowed to communicate, but discussion in Mental Maths sessions explaining how answers are arrived at is vital. The discussion and explanation of the calculation process enables everyone to share and develop their own understanding. This is a fundamental change from rote testing. So as well as being a means of assessing understanding, Mental Maths becomes a place for its teaching. Mental Maths should also be enjoyed. The process of developing mathematics by sharing ideas and developing thinking with teacher and class is distinct from the silence of a mathematics test. Children learn to develop their mathematics in the former: their confidence can be build through understanding and through partnership with others.

Responses to discussion

Discussing strategies for working with numbers can lead to a series of responses from children. By examining these with examples their value in developing mathematical understanding is identified. The common responses examined are:

- a wish to adopt this strategy;
- a choice to refine it further;
- a preference for their existing strategy; and
- the demonstration of a misunderstanding of a specific number issue.

Adopting new strategies

An opportunity for adopting a new strategy occurs when discussing multiplication by 9 (see below).

Multiplying 5 by 9

Child A argues for counting in fives, nine times, and reaches 45 (Figure 2.1). Others agree that this strategy works and provides the correct answer. As discussion is widened for further suggestions Child B offers multiplying by 10 and subtracting 5, which also gives 45 as the answer (Figure 2.2). This strategy can then be discussed for efficiency and reliability with other examples of multiplying with 9. A choice of strategy is now available to the class.

1	2	3	4	**5**	6	7	8	9	**10**	11	12	13	14	**15**
16	17	18	19	**20**	21	22	23	24	**25**	26	27	28	29	**30**
31	32	33	34	**35**	36	37	38	39	**40**	41	42	43	44	**45**

Figure 2.1 Method 1 – counting in fives to calculate 5 × 9

$$5 \times 10 = 50$$
$$50 - 5 = 45$$

Figure 2.2 Method 2 – using known facts (5 × 10) to calculate 5 × 9

The adoption of fresh and more efficient strategies is important in Mental Maths sessions. Such discussions focus on multiplication as a concept and extend it further into the relationships between tables. Further questions involving tables will support future discussion and understanding. These could include: 'Can I get to the four times table by doubling the two times table?' and 'Can I get to the eight times table by doubling the four times table?' Discussion of how answers are derived has great potential for learning. It develops a network of understandings of the number system by identifying, using and developing relationships between understandings. Without discussion, these relationships would not have been identified or used to construct understanding.

Refining strategies

By discussing strategies children may refine strategies further. If mathematics is enjoyable and inspiring this should be expected. One common strategy is to calculate $56 + 27$ as: $(50 + 20) + (6 + 7) = 83$. This strategy is called 'partitioning'. The numbers to be added are partitioned into thousands, hundreds, tens and units as necessary. Using place value in this way allows the calculation to be performed mentally and it is also a basis for initial written calculation in the National Numeracy Strategy. Children will often refine partitioning further (e.g. Figures 2.3 and 2.4). This use of strategies and subsequent refinement can only flourish if regular and frequent time is allocated.

$$
\begin{array}{rl}
\mathbf{1675 + 482} \rightarrow & 1000 + 0 = 1000 \\
& 600 + 400 = 1000 \\
& 70 + 80 = 150 \\
& 5 + 2 = 7 \\
\hline
& 2157
\end{array}
$$

Figure 2.3   Partitioning

$$
\begin{array}{rl}
\mathbf{1675 + 482} \rightarrow & 1675 + 400 = 2075 \\
& 2075 + 82 = 2157
\end{array}
$$

Figure 2.4   Refined partitioning

Preferences for strategies

Children adopt and stick to strategies through either lack of confidence or personal preference. Knowing whether the child makes an informed choice of strategies is essential in differentiating between the two. Children can often be reluctant to adopt more efficient and appropriate strategies because of a lack of confidence. They have a strategy that works and rely on it to the exclusion of other strategies.

Occasionally, having developed the strategy of 'counting on' in their Reception year, children at Key Stage 1 do not develop further strategies for addition in succeeding year groups. Although 'counting on' is wholly appropriate in Reception, it is limiting in subsequent years when working with larger numbers. Experienced teachers tackle issues like this with individual or small group work that builds number confidence. A child in this situation depends on a strategy that excludes the learning of more efficient means of calculation. The strategy is a barrier to mathematical development. In these situations the selection of a strategy is not a matter of informed choice, but of no choice. Children in this predicament often need help to develop their confidence.

Direct intervention with an 'unconfident' child is distinct from a child having a personal preference for a strategy. For example, 136 + 25 can be calculated mentally using a number of strategies, two common ones being 'bridging' and 'partitioning' (Figure 2.5). The issue of how the calculation is performed is less significant than whether it was well managed.

A personal preference for the strategy used in tackling mental calculations is legitimate. The choice of 'partitioning' or 'bridging' or another strategy is a matter of personal selection. A child should be left to select a strategy framed by discussions in class. Issues of appropriateness, suitability and efficiency are relevant and will still need scrutiny, but the choice lies with the child. Generally, children will adopt the most efficient strategies. This does not typically happen on first hearing – time is required for strategies to be adopted. However, if an informed choice to use one strategy rather than another has been made and the strategy works, the selection of that strategy is appropriate. Experience of daily Mental Maths is needed to facilitate the development and refinement of strategies that are appropriate, efficient, suitable and effective, and to ensure their adoption.

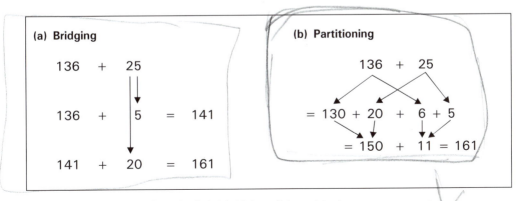

Figure 2.5   A choice of method: (a) bridging; (b) partitioning

Enjoyment stems from developing and personalising strategies. In our experience children enjoy Mental Maths, and its skilful deployment enables mathematics to be taught in ways that give learners and their teacher much satisfaction. But the enjoyment of the process can become problematic because it can disguise the pressure placed on teachers. Paying careful attention to the strategies offered and seizing opportunities to develop understanding make ten minutes of Mental Maths extremely taxing. For this reason it is best to keep to a limit of ten minutes.

Errors with strategies

If children make errors when explaining their strategy, their misconceptions can be identified. For the teacher this information is extremely valuable. Using it effectively is a professional decision for the teacher. The tackling of misconceptions is vital to developing mathematical understanding and the identification and reconstruction of misunderstandings into useable knowledge provide a significant opportunity for learning. Correcting errors and misconceptions uncovered by Mental Maths is crucial in developing effective mental strategies. The Mental Maths of the National Numeracy Strategy is a very powerful learning environment because it develops strategies of mental calculation that build a network of understandings and because it tackles misconceptions as they arise.

Conclusions

In this chapter we have defined and examined the differences between the Mental Maths of the National Numeracy Strategy and more traditional conceptions. The role of discussion in developing children's mathematics is fundamental to this distinction. Using Mental Maths as a lead for discussing strategies and developing understanding is a powerful tool for learning. To use this tool effectively, discussion needs to be purposefully focused with the teacher aware of and responding to the possible outcomes.

In Chapter 3 we examine the classroom management required for Mental Maths. Different mental strategies are explored and classroom ideas are discussed. Without the placing of Mental Maths into a learning context these elements are less effective with children. Full appreciation of why Mental Maths is such a powerful element of the Numeracy Strategy is pivotal when running classroom sessions.

CHAPTER 3
Teaching Mental Maths

Issues surrounding the introduction and nurture of Mental Maths in the classroom are examined in this chapter. In Chapter 2, Mental Maths was discussed in the abstract, but here we look at issues of Mental Maths from the perspective of the classroom, including:

- introducing Mental Maths to a class;
- leading and developing mathematical discussions with a class;
- common mental strategies; and
- Mental Maths case studies.

The experience of running successful Mental Maths sessions is significant for developing expertise. In this chapter we illustrate how this process can begin. In *Number at Key Stage 2*, Mental Maths is placed in context as follows:

> Mental Mathematics encourages children to use numbers flexibly, and to see patterns and relationships. In order to know how children think about numbers, it is important to discuss, share and compare methods, and to expect children to be explicit about their mental images. (Askew *et al.* 1996: ii)

It is crucial to provide an environment that allows discussion to flourish, and it is particularly important when using Mental Maths with a class for the first time.

Introducing Mental Maths to your class

Generalising about classes and children is problematic. Many classes and children will become accustomed, confident and fluent in Mental Maths sessions very quickly. However, as much as these reactions are typical, it is likely that some classes and children will not relish the prospect of being asked to complete calculations in public. Further, children can be intimidated when explaining calculations to their peers. Relationships within a class are an important factor, and it takes time to establish good relationships. Children who know, trust and respect their teacher will be less inhibited discussing mathematics.

Unfortunately this will not be the situation every time Mental Maths is taught. For a variety of reasons teachers can find themselves teaching Mental Maths to children:

- who do not know them well;
- who are nervous of them;
- of whom they have an incomplete picture of ability; or
- whose behaviour is challenging.

The following strategies have helped in situations such as these and with adaptation are useful in a variety of contexts.

Favourite numbers

The purpose of this activity is to develop children's confidence with discussions involving number. It is particularly useful in situations were teacher and class are new to each other. It is an opportunity to discuss numbers and develop a non-threatening environment for deliberation. Initially the teacher narrates a personal story concerning number to the class. The purpose of the story is to generate discussion. Opposite is one that I have used successfully. I begin by asking the class if they have a favourite number. My experience is that most children will not offer one. Even when a child does and they discuss why it's a favourite it still allows the teacher to introduce theirs. This will become the basis for the discussion. Developing a favourite number is significant mathematically for some children, particularly those lacking in confidence with mathematics who have little affection for numbers. The example here is a reflection on childhood experience and may be gender specific.

After the story a period of questioning can begin. The class may ask you questions or wish to share their favourite numbers and thoughts. Managing this discussion and questioning sets the format for future Mental Maths work. Ensuring that all pupils have the opportunity to contribute and that the teacher answers and asks questions are crucial aspects to reinforce. In the next Mental Maths session discussions of favourite numbers may continue. From this point forward a clear format for Mental Maths can develop. Once you have this basis from which to discuss numbers you can move the discussion into calculations speedily with less anxiety for the class.

My favourite numbers

The first World Cup I remember was when I was very tiny. What I remember most about it was the number 10. It was a very long time ago and it was the World Cup that Brazil won for the third time and in it Pele was brilliant! He played in the number 10 shirt and he did such amazing things you wouldn't believe! I remember wishing I could play football like that. The moment I remember best was when somebody passed the ball to him and he shaped to shoot the ball into the goal, but he was so cool that at the last minute he didn't shoot. The goalkeeper thought he was going to and dived to save the shot but it didn't come. Pele left the ball to head towards the goal and because the goalie had already dived he couldn't stop it. Right at the last moment another player came running in to kick the ball off the line and save the goal. I remember very clearly Pele with a blue number 10 on his back and being very disappointed that the goal didn't go in. It could have been the most perfect goal ever scored. Everyone was talking about Pele but it was the number 10 I remember most.

I also have another favourite number. Can I tell you about it? [You are not expecting a no at this point!] A long time later when I was big enough to go to football matches with my friends we went to see Arsenal play Stoke. It wasn't a very exciting game. In fact we had the feeling that it was going to be a dreaded nil–niler. Then Kenny Sanson, who would become my favourite player, did two great things. First he ran down the wing and took the ball past a couple of players and crossed the ball over for a goal. I think John Hollins scored but I can't be certain. What a relief – a goal! Then, just before the end, Kenny scored. My friends and I were just behind the goal when the ball was crossed into the penalty area and Kenny rose and headed the ball right into the back of the net. I can still remember him turning and running away from the goal with the number 3 on his shirt facing the goal.

These are my two favourite numbers: 10 and 3.

Initial mental calculation

A number of good ideas develop calculating strategies. One excellent exercise, which works equally well at home or in the classroom, develops like this. Ask the children to shut their eyes and picture eight white discs in a line. Then ask them to make sure there are eight by counting them. Next have them put the discs into groups of two and ask, 'How many groups are there?'. The results should be discussed so that the various mental pictures are revealed. You can then progress to groups of four. This generates some more discussion with the right questioning. A good way to finish is to ask the class to put the discs into groups of three and inquire what problems they have doing that.

This activity can be modified for children of different ages and abilities. Very young children can use the discs for developing initial mental strategies. Older children can discuss the relationship between multiplication and division linked with remainders. This is useful even when children have a good mathematical grounding. It is valuable to this group because of the discussion it provokes. As such, the usefulness of most Mental Maths activities depends on the discussion they generate.

Leading and developing mathematical discussions with a class

Open and closed questions are two principal tools for developing discussion (Figure 3.1). Both are useful but make different demands of pupils. When used in combination they are very powerful.

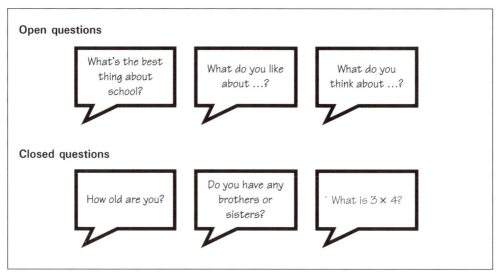

Figure 3.1   Open and closed questions

Using open questions

Open questions allow for a range of responses. Responses to the question, 'What's the best thing about school?' depend on experience and opinion. Possible responses include: 'Being with my friends', or 'I enjoy Maths', or even 'lunchtime's good' or 'home time'. The last two responses may not be helpful in generating a discussion of school. They are not wrong but they do not offer the profitable opportunities for examination of the others. Open questions can sometimes elicit responses that are unhelpful for discussion. To elicit profitable responses teacher and class must share an understanding of pertinence. Pupils' ability to formulate appropriate responses to open questions stems from an understanding of their context and why the question is being asked. Developing pertinent responses requires assessable questions and awareness of good responses.

Responses to open questions can be further categorised. Responding 'Because we go on the space shuttle!' to the original question falls outside school experience, making it inappropriate. Once an understanding of pertinence is shared between teachers and pupils, open questions become pivotal to discussion in Mental Maths.

The activity 'What makes a bad answer' is drawn from a series of discussions we have used in school. Exploring *good* responses is useful for Mental Maths. It is extremely important with a new class. Equally, one can learn from the opposite situation and explore bad answers. In the discussion that follows the class will identify and discuss features of bad answers. By doing so the importance of context is demonstrated.

What makes a bad answer?

After some initial discussion of what makes a good answer, ask a problematic open question: 'What would be a bad answer to "how do I get to the head teacher's office from our classroom?"' Depending on age and ability responses to this question will vary. It is likely, however, that the issues raised in the discussion will be real issues for the class; issues that stem from their experience of questioning. After dealing with clearly wrong answers – giving directions to the kitchen, etc. – lead the conversation to explore the not factually wrong but the longwinded. Going via the corner shop need not eventually be wrong but is it the best answer?

Different responses may be equally valid, giving two or more right answers. Once this has been established ask the children to devise their 'best bad but right answers' and then discuss the merits of each. Vitally, this makes awareness of what the questioner is looking for crucial. It further identifies a bad answer as one not providing the questioner with what they were seeking, developing context as an issue. Once this issue has been established it needs identification in as many different classroom situations as possible. Making this a persistent issue for thought and discussion for children develops their responses.

The profitable use of open questions requires the teacher and the class to have a shared understanding of the process. Open questioning promotes class participation. It encourages and nourishes broad mathematical thinking, which, in turn builds mathematical connections between understandings through the discussion of issues raised. Consider the following open question: 'I have 183 pupils to take on a school trip. I can take 50 pupils in a coach and 20 pupils on a minibus. How many vehicles do I need?' This will promote a variety of answers, some of which are right (three coaches and two minibuses), some of which are right but inappropriate (ten minibuses) and some which are wrong (five coaches). The questions in Figure 3.2 are useful for developing discussion.

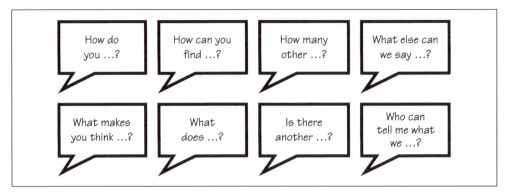

Figure 3.2   Open questions

Further issues

Children can respond to open questions involving mental calculation with, 'My brain told me', or 'I guessed'. This can be evidence of either not understanding what is being demanded of them or a desire not to share their thoughts with the class. Replies like these need examination. Children that do not wish to respond in class discussion should not be forced to. This would be counterproductive to them as mathematics learners and may detract from the developing discussion. They can be encouraged to contribute by developing confidence and emphasising the non-threatening nature of the discussion. For Mental Maths sessions to work effectively, those who are shy or lacking in confidence need to be included at their own pace.

A further issue facing teachers is the genuine desire of some children to turn Mental Maths into a competitive race to be the first to answer. Such desires often stem from a will to please and a need to demonstrate skill. This need is acute in some children. These situations must, however, be tackled. They can de-motivate other children who are not yet as rapid with their calculations. The goal of Mental Maths is to have the whole class actively engaged in discussions, not just the able. The able will have the opportunities to demonstrate their skill and frequently this will benefit all. Mental Maths needs managing so that all take part in the process.

Using closed questioning

Open questions have further limitations for teaching. Sometimes pupils will not draw the conclusions sought in discussions. There will be times when questions like, 'What do you think is happening?' will not bring a desired response. In these situations asking narrower closed questions will develop the understanding sought. Closed questioning can make explicit exactly what the teacher is seeking. They provide direction for thinking. This is illustrated by the example opposite concerning commutativity.

Discussion of commutativity

Teacher: What do you notice about the answers to multiplication questions?

Child: They are always the same.

Teacher: Does everybody agree?

Class: Yes.

Teacher: What do you mean by always the same?

Child: 3 times 4 is always 12.

Teacher: Can you say anything else about multiplying 3 and 4?

Child: 3 lots of 4 is always 12.

At this point in the discussion the class need further direction. Open questioning has not enabled commutativity to be recognised in this context.

Teacher: What do 4 lots of 3 make?

Child: 12.

Teacher: What do 3 lots of 4 make?

Child: 12.

Teacher: So is it right that 3 multiplied by 4 makes 12 and that 4 multiplied by 3 makes 12?

Class: Yes!

Teacher: Does it matter which way round the 3 and 4 are when multiplying them?

Class: No.

Teacher: What else can you now say about multiplication questions?

Discussion moves onto commutativity.

Using closed questions is a successful teaching strategy when used within a framework of open questioning. If children are to generalise from closed questioning finishing the dialogue with an open question is beneficial. In the example above the final open question is an invitation to test the freshly acquired understanding by having pupils:

- explain what their understanding is; or
- test the findings for themselves.

Closed questions do not develop a learning dialogue in Mental Maths sessions. Their success is due to the way they focus attention on specific issues under discussion. Used like this they are a powerful teaching tool. If overused in discussion they develop little more than rote learning and their effect is diminished.

Using both open and closed questions is important for the development of Mental Maths. Open questions encourage children to respond in discussion and think broadly. Closed questions will often focus attention on specific issues and allow children to draw conclusions that develop their understanding. As the two are combined they develop a powerful discursive environment for the teaching of mathematics.

Managing discussion

Strategies to encourage reflection and inclusion involve allowing everyone personal thinking time. This can be achieved by not allowing any responses for a brief period, e.g. allowing hands up only when you raise yours. This gives time for the teacher to introduce some clues and for the less rapid to become involved. Slightly slowing the discussion allows it to become more inclusive. There are also a number of resources that increase inclusion. The use of digit cards and number fans help to ensure that the entire class prepares a response, not just those selected by the teacher. This also provides an assessment opportunity. At such times, the most significant point is to note the pupils who are waiting for their peers' responses before offering their own.

Using these resources effectively requires coordination of all responses with cards or fans. The 'one, two, three, show' system is an effective way to coordinate responses. Not only does it set the pace of discussion but also it gives the teacher greater control of the process. It is also a subtle way to provide thinking ('take up') time for the class. After setting a calculation a count to three will provide enough calculation time. After a number of responses have been made, open questions are used to explore them. The questions in Figure 3.2 are useful for this.

Mental Maths need not always follow a rigid structure. Once a basis for Mental Maths has been established adaptations will be needed periodically. These are required for two main reasons:

- the Mental Maths component of a lesson may be used to introduce new concepts requiring more time; and
- the existing format may not suit an area to be covered.

However, without a basic structure which can be adapted, teaching and learning through Mental Maths is more problematic. Providing a structure which all participants are aware of allows discussion to be more easily managed.

- **Rearranging numbers**
  8 + 41 is more easily calculated by 41 + 8.
  Recognise that some number problems are commutative.

- **Using repeated operations**
  Find $\frac{1}{9}$ by finding $\frac{1}{3}$ of $\frac{1}{3}$.

- **Halving and doubling**
  $18 \times 4 = 9 \times 8$
  15% of 40 can be calculated by finding 10% of 40 = 4. Now half of
  the 10% (i.e. 5%) is 2. So 15% of 40 is 4 + 2 = 6.

- **Using near doubles or halves**
  $25 + 26 = (25 \times 2) + 1$ or $(26 \times 2) - 1$

- **Using similar patterns and calculations**
  $25 \times 4 = 100$ so $26 \times 4 = (25 \times 4) + 4$
  Work on the 4 times table by doubling 2, or the 8 times table by
  doubling 4.

- **Partitioning**
  $45 + 26 = (40 + 20) + (5 + 6) = 71$

- **Bridging**
  Use knowledge of the nearest 10.
  Thus 136 + 25 becomes $136 + 5 + 20 = 141 + 20 = 161$.

Figure 3.3   The magnificent seven (adapted from DfEE 1998)

Common mental strategies

Using common mental strategies and allowing children to develop and personalise them will engender enjoyment of Mental Maths, but the choice of mental strategy does raise some issues (see Chapter 2). Efficiency is key in the selection of a strategy. The mental strategies in Figure 3.3 have been characterised as the 'magnificent seven'. This is not an exhaustive list but it identifies a key issue in using mental strategies. The criteria for selecting a strategy should focus on whether:

- the strategy works; and
- the strategy is efficient.

From the strategies identified in Figure 3.3 many choices in calculation are available but when pupils select a strategy, efficiency should be an important consideration. For example, the calculation 25 + 26 can be performed using a number of different strategies. Using the criterion of efficiency, 'near doubles' is the quickest:

$$25 + 26 = (25 \times 2) + 1$$

or

$$25 + 26 = (26 \times 2) - 1$$

Other strategies are generally more time consuming and less efficient. For example, using partitioning:

$$20 + 5 + 20 + 6 = (20 + 20) + (5 + 6) = 40 + (11) = 51$$

The greater number of steps required using partitioning for this calculation make it less suitable than 'near doubles'.

As the number of strategies available to children increases, their choice of strategy should stem from efficiency. Personal preference will also be a factor but as Mental Maths experience increases, confidence that strategies work increases to the point where selection stems from efficiency. There will be instances when the selection of the most efficient strategy is unclear, and these often make good points of discussion.

The selection of strategy and the discussion that selection creates become increasingly developed as more strategies are acquired by pupils. As the number of strategies in use increases, the importance of efficiency escalates. Once a connection is made between efficiency and appropriateness, discussions of strategies progress further. The selection of an appropriate strategy involves:

- correctly applying a working strategy; and
- selecting an efficient strategy.

These criteria establish profitable discussions. Pupils will still exercise choice over strategies and this will mean that sometimes a less efficient method is selected. However, once efficiency is identified in the process of selecting strategies such instances should decline.

Mental Maths case studies

There now follow some examples of Mental Maths activities from a range of ages and contexts. These are teacher accounts of sessions that have been slightly modified for clarity and to keep them brief. In the first example the teacher links the activity included in the Mental Maths session with work in the main part of the lesson.

The activity in Case Study 1 is interesting because it tackles an issue that will be faced by a number of early years teachers – pupils not enjoying answering direct questions. By working on this activity the children still engage with the questions but they become less threatening. There was also a purpose to the learning of number bonds – being able to perform tricks!

In Case Study 2, counting is used as a basis for Mental Maths.

In the examination of a Year 5/6 class the issue of noise is also present. In Case Study 3, number fans are used with the whole class. Two clear issues arise from this case study. The first is clearly wider school organisation. Large enthusiastic classes

Case Study 1

The class

The class consists of 28 Year 2 children of mixed ability and from generally low-income families. The children have some experience of Mental Maths and enjoy the social interaction it fosters. They can become a handful and the social side of all activities needs managing. They are also initially less enthusiastic about direct questions.

Learning objectives
- Reinforce and practice number bonds to ten.
- Develop algebraic thinking by working with unknown numbers.

The activity

I had seen this idea on an INSET course, or something like that. It's the one where you make up a set of cards to reinforce number bonds. On one side of the card you place one part of a number bond and on the other its partner. So if you place a 3 on one side the other side has a 7 and so on. I included 0 and 10. To start the activity I placed all the cards on the carpet while they stood up and watched.

I began with, 'I know what's on the back of that card – you see the number 4'. After a few examples were proved I asked whether anyone could spot how I did it. I wanted the class to engage with the activity and share their ideas on how I knew the number on the back of each card. I asked lots of open questions and even when the solution to the riddle was uncovered there were still opportunities to discuss how you knew 7 was on the back of 3. The children became quite good at counting on in different steps to check whether their answer was correct. I was surprised by how long it took for the class to spot the pattern. My use of questioning helped to make this clear.

The teacher's comments

We had some good discussion for checking number bonds. Counting in different steps to work out what was on the back of cards was common. Many children had a sound grasp of number bonds so often I was told, 'I just know'. When I asked them how they would check to make sure they were right, other strategies were given.

On this occasion I wanted to carry on working with number bonds after Mental Maths had finished. To achieve this I gave all the groups the task of making cards. Two groups set about making 'number bonds to 10' cards while some with primary support just completed 'number bonds to 5'. My top group worked on 'spider cards'. These work in the same way but 8 (the spider's legs) is added to numbers up to 15 (number bonds to 23).

The cards proved useful for discussion much later. By all accounts, when they went home the mathematics continued there with family members.

Case Study 2

The class

The class consists of 25 less able Year 3 children, all with English as a first language. although about 30 per cent of them are American. The class is small due to the setting policy of the school, which allows smaller sets for the weaker pupils. The most able group contained 36 children in the same year group.

Learning objectives

- Children should be able to count on and back in steps of any size.
- Children should recognise odd and even numbers.

The activity

The children were seated in a circle after the register has been called. The class was then asked to count round in the circle to 100 in twos. When they had finished they counted backwards. The same activity was then repeated with fives and tens. The class was then challenged to set a record to see how quickly they could count in fives to 100. The attempt was timed. I then challenged the class to beat this time.

The class was reminded of odd and even numbers before being challenged to count forwards in threes. They were told to stand up if their number was even and not to take any further part in the counting. The game ended when all the children were standing up. Finally the children played this game against the clock.

This concluded the Mental Maths part of the lesson. However, two of the five groups went on to practice further during the main part of the lesson. They investigated what happened to the 'odd or evenness' when numbers were doubled.

The teacher's comments

I was very pleased with how well this lesson went. The small class size may have allowed the lesson to run more smoothly than it might have done with a larger group. The class really enjoyed racing to beat their record for counting around the circle.

I planned and carried out further activities in this session. This was only possible because of the children's prior experience of Mental Maths. I find that starting the session with something that the children have previously experienced helps boost their confidence during the rest of the lesson, and it revises and refines their skills.

Having the children stand up when their number was even worked: they enjoyed the activity whether their answer was right or wrong. This stemmed from the class being very supportive of each other. With different children, this sort of activity might require rethinking, particularly when the children are new to Mental Maths. The movement of standing up seems to help stop children fidgeting and maintains concentration, but it can be noisy.

Case Study 3

The class

The class consists of 35 middle to lower ability children in a mixed Year 5/6 class. About 50 per cent of the children have English as an additional language (EAL). The school has a mixed catchment area with approximately 50 per cent of the school having free meals. The class is very enthusiastic and keen to contribute orally. The school is semi-open plan and this, combined with the children's enthusiasm, has been problematic in the past as noise disturbs other classes. The class has also had some problems appreciating the Mental Maths component of numeracy lessons. Children had commented on missing ticks in their mathematics books and the feeling of success that this brought.

Learning objectives

- Children should be able to count on and back in repeated steps of 1, 10, 100, 1000.
- Children should develop competence at putting the largest number first to simplify the addition of larger numbers.

The activity

Due to the limited space the class were seated at their desks facing the front. They had access to number fans placed on their tables. I reminded the class about the rules for using number fans and the procedure within the class for answering questions. I have used the 'one, two, three, show' procedure. Next I examined counting on as a strategy for adding numbers and discussed with the class counting on in larger steps. We then counted up to 500 in tens and then to 5,000 in hundreds. I asked questions they could respond to with their number fans: 'Show me' ... 60 + 10, 10 + 60, 120 + 20, 20 + 120, 1000 + 200, 200 + 1000, etc. I stopped the class to discuss which of the calculations were the easiest and why. I selected a child and discussed why it is easier to add on a number when you only have a few numbers to count on. I widened the discussion and helped the class to experience this for themselves by asking them to count aloud to show 20 + 70 and then 70 + 20. I was surprised that their experiences with smaller numbers hadn't prepared them for this.

The teacher's comments

This was a very large class and awkward at times. The lesson needed to be very structured to maintain order. I was pleased that the group had started to gain confidence in answering questions and the security developed using number fans or digit cards had helped further this. The sharing of strategies helped to encourage the children to value the contributions they all made during the lesson. The enthusiasm of the children may have consequences in terms of noise. This may be partly due to relaxed discipline but tighter control inhibits discussion. I cannot see any easy answers to this issue. Without control a teacher is ineffective and this does not help numeracy teaching. Timetabling might tackle some of these issues. For example, if the classes in the vicinity carried out similar Mental Maths activities, then disturbances would reduce. There would simply be a buzzy noise during Mental Maths.

combined with an awkward school layout for Mental Maths will create some problems. Timetabling may be a partial solution but there will be examples where this will not work. Crucially, issues like this are wider school issues. Individual class teachers or parents may not have the power to resolve them. Tackling these issues as a whole school is the only way to resolve them. The example of noise is not the only one that needs tackling; resourcing, support staff time and parent help are also wider issues.

The second issue that stems from the comments of the Year 5/6 teacher are children who miss the reassurance that a page of ticks can bring. That a page of correctly answered sums can hide a multitude of misunderstanding and misconceptions is not the issue here. The issue is that some positive feelings about mathematics stem from clear signs of success. For children to feel successful they need evidence of this. This is often an issue for EAL children. Our experience of such children is that they often have excellent skills in written calculation. It may also be a significant area of success in school.

Mental Maths is both a mental and an oral process. The double whammy of removing opportunity for success by doing less written work and increasing exclusion through increased oral work may have a negative effect. Increased oral work should help the EAL child because it should develop language skills along with numeracy, but this will not be automatic. Those involved – teacher, parent and child – will have to work extremely hard to bring success. Awareness is paramount in situations like this.

Feelings of success

The National Numeracy Strategy should change the way mathematics is taught. It is more concerned with everyone achieving than with the success of a few. Part of this process involves children publicly demonstrating their skill. National Numeracy Strategy videos often give nice examples of children demonstrating their mathematics publicly: taking tables tests in front of their peers or explaining an unusual strategy. The difference in this approach compared to the old style of teaching is that all the children have the opportunity to shine. Success need not be measured in terms of 'where I came in the class' but 'how well everyone has done'. This does not mean that the mathematically gifted are held back – all the evidence points away from this conclusion – but it does allow all to feel some success in mathematics. Although this has yet to be fully researched, the widened feeling of achievement brought about by the National Numeracy Strategy may be one of the reasons it succeeds, but the major factor will be the hard work of the teachers implementing it daily.

CHAPTER 4
The 'new' written methods

In this chapter we examine written methods of the National Numeracy Strategy. Examples of actual calculations are included and annotated. These details identify the crucial understandings required to develop fluent and accurate written calculation in addition, subtraction, multiplication and division.

The National Numeracy Strategy has two goals for written methods. Firstly, it promotes the traditional, efficient and common formal written methods as goals for Year 6. A second goal is that children understand the process of written calculations. This means that teaching written calculation is more than a rote learning of rules to be applied. Children must understand the process behind calculations. This is the significant shift. Previously, even the successful child may have grasped nothing but a list of rules to follow. Over the four years of Key Stage 2, understanding how and why written processes work will be crucial. In this chapter we examine written methods and identify how each new method develops understanding. Written methods are used to develop wider mathematical understanding rather than promote rule following.

The National Numeracy Strategy structures the development of the teaching of written methods across Key Stage 2. This adds clarity to the charged issue of formal sums or algorithms, which can be a barrier to many children's mathematical understanding. Using formal algorithms children often make errors, which produce answers that are mathematically nonsensical. Figure 4.1 shows a common example.

Rule following or rote learning is a common element of traditional mathematics teaching. Instances like the example in Figure 4.1 highlight its failings. In this example the child's weakness in understanding is much deeper than simply not following a crucial rule. Errors such as this point to a lack of understanding of place value. This understanding of how numbers operate is a vital mathematical awareness.

Problems with place value become increasingly evident as the rules required in calculations get more complicated. Decomposition, a formal method of subtraction, often presents children and adults with problems. This is particularly marked with a calculation involving a run of zeros. Figure 4.2 shows first how the calculation 'should' be carried out, followed by two examples of common problems.

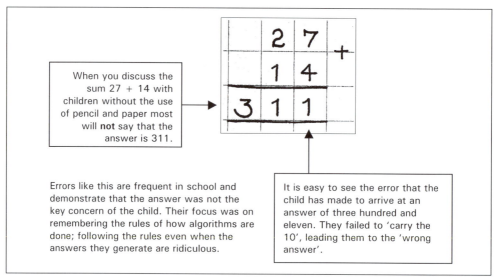

When you discuss the sum 27 + 14 with children without the use of pencil and paper most will **not** say that the answer is 311.

Errors like this are frequent in school and demonstrate that the answer was not the key concern of the child. Their focus was on remembering the rules of how algorithms are done; following the rules even when the answers they generate are ridiculous.

It is easy to see the error that the child has made to arrive at an answer of three hundred and eleven. They failed to 'carry the 10', leading them to the 'wrong answer'.

Figure 4.1   A common error in addition

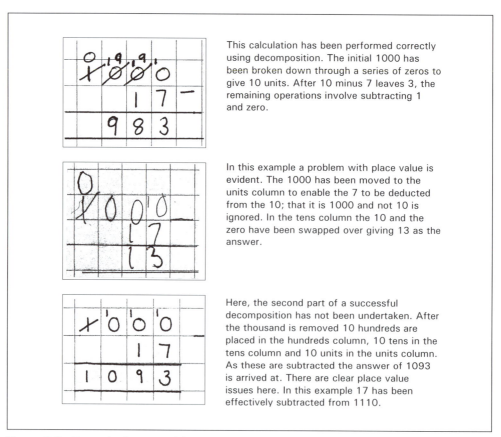

This calculation has been performed correctly using decomposition. The initial 1000 has been broken down through a series of zeros to give 10 units. After 10 minus 7 leaves 3, the remaining operations involve subtracting 1 and zero.

In this example a problem with place value is evident. The 1000 has been moved to the units column to enable the 7 to be deducted from the 10; that it is 1000 and not 10 is ignored. In the tens column the 10 and the zero have been swapped over giving 13 as the answer.

Here, the second part of a successful decomposition has not been undertaken. After the thousand is removed 10 hundreds are placed in the hundreds column, 10 tens in the tens column and 10 units in the units column. As these are subtracted the answer of 1093 is arrived at. There are clear place value issues here. In this example 17 has been effectively subtracted from 1110.

Figure 4.2   Errors in decomposition

When only the rules for completing written calculations are taught, an understanding of *why* can become removed from the process, because it is just not seen as necessary for effective calculation. In the worst examples this can be catastrophic for understanding mathematics, which simply becomes rote learning of increasingly complex steps.

Since a clear understanding of place value is not required to complete formal written calculations children do not have the opportunity to develop this essential understanding. Successfully completing pages of sums often only identifies the correct application of rules. It cannot be taken as evidence of sound mathematical understanding; it provides no basis upon which to judge place value. Children that do not develop a sound appreciation of place value find later mathematical development difficult. We shall return to the consequences of this in the conclusion.

Learning formal written methods

Formal algorithms are extremely efficient methods of written calculation, which means they are very powerful tools. Before we had calculators and computers, most commerce was conducted using these algorithms. The educational problem with using algorithms is that they hide the important mathematical principles of how they work. The National Numeracy Strategy does not aim to eradicate these methods but rather to delay their introduction until children have grasped fundamental principles such as place value. When the learning of written methods assists the development and understanding of place value children's mathematical proficiency is enhanced considerably.

Children will begin learning formal efficient methods from Year 4. Before this, focused activities, increased Mental Maths teaching and informal written methods or jottings will develop understanding of place value. These jottings make mathematical processes more transparent and identify how correct answers are derived. Before we examine some examples, three issues surrounding the use of informal written methods must be examined.

- *Methods initially built on mental methods*
  Strategies used for Mental Maths will play a major part in the development of written strategies. Children fluent and competent with Mental Maths will adapt these skills in written calculations, thus making the calculation process clearer.

- *Calculations involve partitioning not digits*
  Initial calculations will involve working with numbers by partitioning. For example, 421 will be worked on not as '4-2-1' but as '400, 20 and 1'. This places much greater emphasis on place value. In traditional methods where all digits are afforded equal status their real value is not linked to obtaining the correct

answer; all numbers are treated as single digits. By employing partitioning initially the value of each part of the number will be crucial to an effective calculation.

- *Calculations do not start with units*
  Written calculation will not start with units until formal methods begin to appear from Year 4. This allows the value of each digit to be emphasised and links place value with mental strategies, which also work this way.

Informal written methods of addition and subtraction in Year 3

Addition

The National Numeracy Strategy offers two methods for addition in Year 3. The first is based upon empty number lines using 'counting on'. This method works with larger numbers but in Figure 4.3 tens and units are the focus. Children will be familiar with 'counting on' as a common mental strategy. This method is particularly effective when used on larger numbers (Figure 4.4).

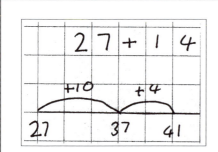

This is the calculation used in Figure 4.1, in which the answer reached was 311. Completing it using this method encourages thought about the numbers involved. It also enables the use of existing mental strategies. Clearly it is more efficient to add the smaller number to the greater and count on.

Figure 4.3 Addition using 'counting on', Year 3

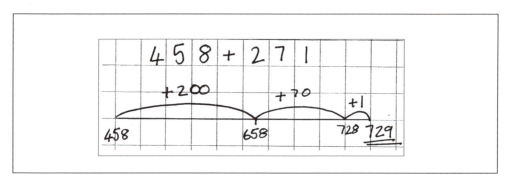

Figure 4.4 Addition using 'counting on', Year 3

Because of their simplicity, jottings like this can easily be performed using an empty number line. The same calculation using traditional tens and units sums may not have even been attempted in Year 3. Using formal methods involving 'carrying' in the tens column, makes this calculation awkward for those new to the method; even less common are calculations involving 'carrying' across all three columns. These calculations are more straightforward using this informal method.

Calculations like this have additional advantages. The route to the answer is transparent; it draws upon previously developed Mental Maths skills in a new context. Further, the value of hundreds, tens and units is pivotal, reinforcing Mental Maths skills and understanding of place value.

During Year 3, children should begin to develop experience of more efficient methods. These will again focus on place value. The children will start by adding the tens column first (Figure 4.5).

Calculations like this begin to develop a passage of learning which will be complete when efficient traditional written methods become dominant. This method still reinforces place value. Tens are treated not as single digits but as tens, in this case 30 and 40. When the addition of units creates a ten it is placed directly into the tens column. When coping with larger numbers place value is again reinforced (Figure 4.6).

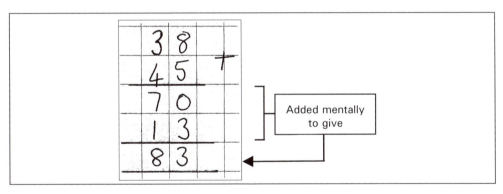

Figure 4.5 Addition, adding the tens column first, Year 3

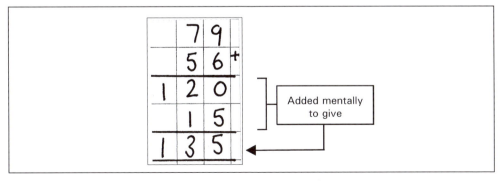

Figure 4.6 Addition, adding the tens column first, Year 3

In practising calculations like these, discussions of place value with children are paramount. In the example in Figure 4.6, hundreds becomes a focus. Calculations like this are more problematic with formal methods, which would require the child to carry successfully twice to reach 135. Written calculations with larger numbers begin in Year 4.

Subtraction

Formal written procedures for subtraction are more awkward than those for addition. This is also true of the informal methods in the National Numeracy Strategy. This increased difficulty is minimal, however, when compared to the jump in formal methods on moving from addition to subtraction.

The first example (Figure 4.7) builds on skills developed with addition. In our classrooms this method (complementary addition) was called 'taking away by adding'. It uses 'counting on' with an empty number line. This method can also be used with larger numbers (Figure 4.8). This promotes place value and builds on mental methods. Both these calculations can also be completed without an empty number line.

The National Numeracy Strategy wants children to use formal methods from a position of strength, so the processes behind them need to be made clear. This can be achieved through the teaching of a variety of strategies. The ultimate goal of such strategies is the preferred use of formal methods, with understanding.

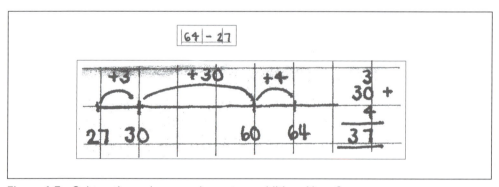

Figure 4.7   Subtraction using complementary addition, Year 3

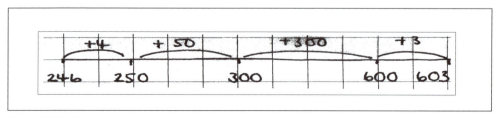

Figure 4.8   Subtraction using complementary addition, Year 3

The move to a mixture of written calculations is important. Here are the two previous examples completed differently (Figures 4.9, 4.10). They still work using complimentary addition and then totalling the difference, but they also begin to emphasise the importance of layout to the calculation. The National Numeracy Strategy includes three pencil and paper methods for subtraction in Year 3. Children should develop familiarity with them all and discuss their merits. Figure 4.10 shows a second written strategy based on a different mental method. The final method (Figure 4.11)

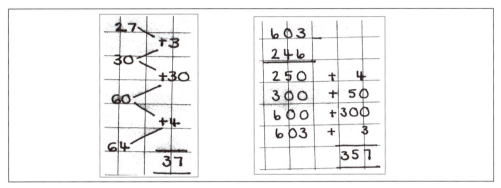

Figure 4.9   Subtraction using complementary addition, Year 3

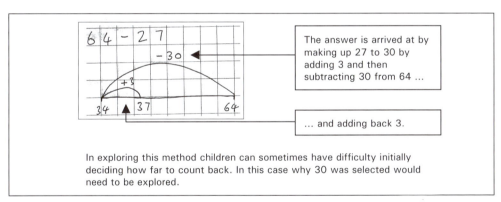

Figure 4.10   Subtraction using compensation, Year 3

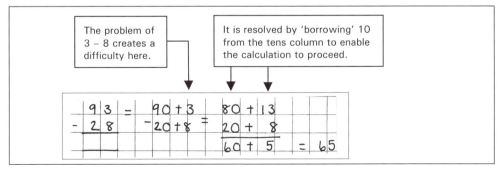

Figure 4.11   Subtraction using decomposition, Year 3

uses decomposition. It introduces an extended version to develop an understanding of the basis of decomposition. Working with this extended form of decomposition places the efficient formal calculation into a learning context. In this example it is clear why and from where tens, hundreds, etc. are taken. In use you will borrow either 10 or 100, avoiding the confusion of always 'borrowing' 1 regardless of real value. This is a far firmer foundation than rote learning and again it ensures that children examine and correctly use place value.

Multiplication and division are developed in Year 3 through Mental Maths. These understandings are significant and prepare children for work on written methods with multiplication and division in Years 4 to 6.

Written methods in Years 4 to 6

The key principles of written methods in the National Numeracy Strategy that have been established so far are that they:

- are based on mental methods;
- develop and enhance place value as a concept; and
- aim to develop understanding that promotes efficient use of formal methods.

Addition

The written methods for addition outlined in Year 4 continue until Year 6. The numbers involved become greater across the year groups and decimals are increasingly used. It is expected that all three methods for addition will continue in each year group and the selection of method will largely depend on the numbers involved. The three methods do not alter as children move from Year 4 to Year 6, but the numbers they are applied to increase (see Table 4.1). Examples from Year 4 are examined here but the same methods should be used with larger numbers in other year groups. The methods illustrated here (Figures 4.12–4.15) are named and annotated.

Table 4.1 Written calculations in Key Stage 2 for addition

Year 3	Year 4	Year 5	Year 6
TU + TU	HTU + TU	HTU + HTU	ThHTU + ThHTU
leading to	leading to	leading to	leading to
HTU + TU	HTU + HTU	ThHTU + ThHTU	any calculations
or HTU + HTU	Begin work on	Use decimals in	with any number
Using two written	decimals with	a wider context	of digits. Continue
methods.	money.	in calculation.	work with decimals.
	Use three	Use three written	Use three written
	written methods.	methods.	methods.

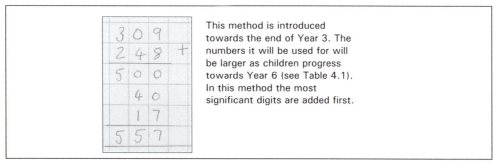

This method is introduced towards the end of Year 3. The numbers it will be used for will be larger as children progress towards Year 6 (see Table 4.1). In this method the most significant digits are added first.

Figure 4.12   Addition by adding the most significant digits first, Years 4–6

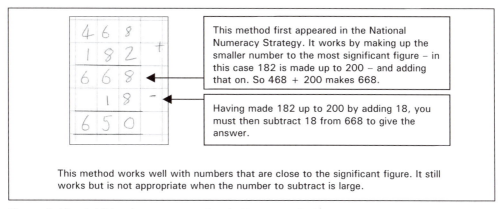

This method first appeared in the National Numeracy Strategy. It works by making up the smaller number to the most significant figure – in this case 182 is made up to 200 – and adding that on. So 468 + 200 makes 668.

Having made 182 up to 200 by adding 18, you must then subtract 18 from 668 to give the answer.

This method works well with numbers that are close to the significant figure. It still works but is not appropriate when the number to subtract is large.

Figure 4.13   Addition by compensation (add too much then take off), Years 4–6

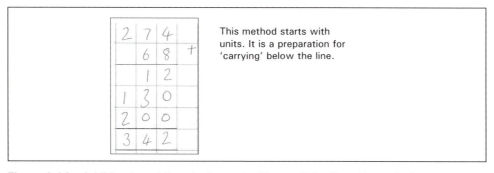

This method starts with units. It is a preparation for 'carrying' below the line.

Figure 4.14   Addition by adding the least significant digits first, Years 4–6

In Year 4, 'carrying' below the line for addition should become one of the methods used. This is a preparation for other years and is the first formal method to be established.

Figure 4.15   Addition by 'carrying' below the line, Years 4–6

The calculation in Figure 4.14 is a key step. It should be introduced over Year 4 and leads to using the standard formal methods. The first stage is to begin working from the right with the units. The move away from empty number lines makes the correct lining up of columns – tens, units, etc. – vital. These calculations are not possible if numbers are incorrectly aligned.

Subtraction

In most respects, written methods of subtraction progress similarly to addition in the National Numeracy Strategy. There are three methods, which are similar in each year group but are applied to increasingly larger numbers. The exception to this is formal decomposition, which is not fully established until Year 6 (see Table 4.2).

The following calculations (Figures 4.16–4.20) are in the order in which they appear in the National Numeracy Strategy. Their workings and issues that they raise have been annotated. The calculation in Figure 4.17 is performed using compensation; take too much and add back. This method would also have been completed using an empty number line in Year 3. The discipline of placing columns correctly is crucial. Also vital is that the method is used on appropriate numbers. The calculation is easiest when the number to be taken away is close to the next significant figure, in this case 78. Adding 22 is very straightforward thereafter. Since most children find addition an easier skill than subtraction, using addition to subtract like this and in the previous method allows more children to work successfully.

Decomposition and an understanding of the process are difficult to develop together, and through Years 4–6 this is achieved through following a number of steps. It is initially a lengthy process until the formal method is introduced in Year 6. The calculation in Figure 4.18 will be used to demonstrate all the forms of decomposition in the National Numeracy Strategy.

Table 4.2   Written calculations in Key Stage 2 for subtraction

Year 3	Year 4	Year 5	Year 6
TU – TU	HTU – TU	HTU – HTU	ThHTU – ThHTU
leading to	leading to	leading to	leading to
HTU – TU	HTU – HTU	ThHTU – ThHTU	calculations with any
or HTU – HTU	Begin work on	Use decimals in a	number of digits.
Use three written	decimals with	wider context in	Continue work with
methods.	money. Continue	calculation. Continue	decimals. Continue
	with three	with three	with three
	methods.	methods.	methods.

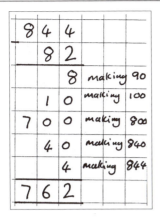

This method was first introduced in Year 3. It was initially developed using an empty number line so that a child has the image of making up to the target number; in this case 844. It now also requires the discipline of aligning columns correctly.

As experience develops the number of jumps can reduce. In this example 18 could be the first step rather than 8 and then 10. Equally 44 could have been added to replace the final two steps rather than 40 and then 4. Crossing tens like this is a key development. It is possible to further reduce the steps to two by adding 718 and then 44.

Figure 4.16 Subtraction using complementary addition, Years 4–6

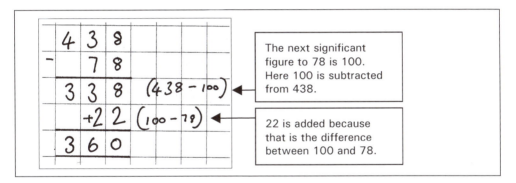

The next significant figure to 78 is 100. Here 100 is subtracted from 438.

22 is added because that is the difference between 100 and 78.

Figure 4.17 Subtraction using compensation, 'take too much and add back', Years 4–6

In Figure 4.18 the process of decomposition is extended so that its operation is clearer, promoting understanding. It should be taught as a single process, and not as a list of steps to be memorised. The key to the process is that where difficult numbers to subtract occur, breaking off some of the larger neighbouring number and adding it to its neighbour in 'difficulty' solves the problem. This is further illustrated in Figure 4.19. Once the process is understood it can be made progressively more efficient. The next step in this process will not partition numbers so overtly. This four-step process could be made into a three-step process by combining the separate steps tackling the units and tens. However, children reaching this level are likely to benefit from the formal method.

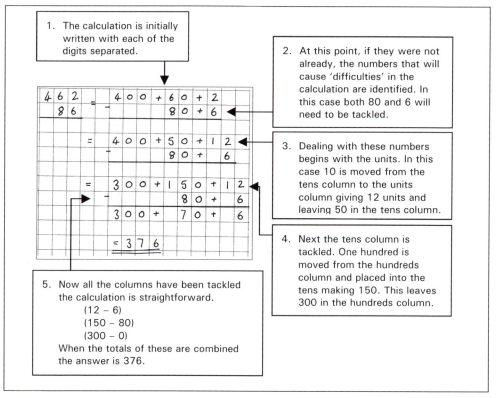

Figure 4.18   Subtraction using decomposition, 1, Years 4–6

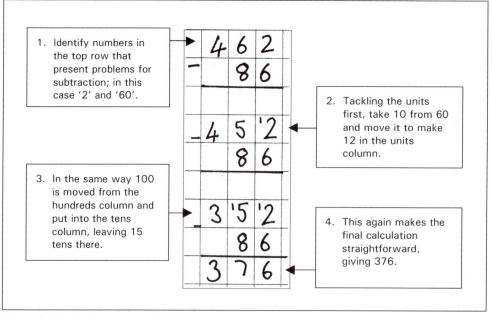

Figure 4.19   Subtraction using decomposition, 2, Years 4–6

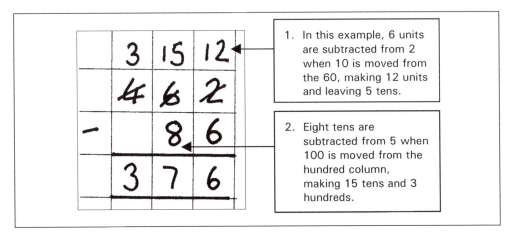

Figure 4.20   Subtraction using decomposition, 3, Years 4–6

The next subtraction (Figure 4.20) is the efficient formal method. It is a slight adaptation from its first appearance in Figure 4.2. In this version the changes made to the tackled numbers are written in full above them and the original is crossed out.

Developing the written skills of subtraction in this way places the goal of accurate written calculation with an understanding of the process behind it within the reach of most children. The other benefit is that throughout the learning process understandings of place value are also developed.

Multiplication

The National Numeracy Strategy has two methods of written calculation for Year 4 to Year 6 (see Table 4.3). The second of these methods also has an adaptation as experience of it grows. In Years 5 and 6 multiplication is applied to decimal and mixed decimal fractions. An important aspect of both methods is approximating the answer before proceeding. This is an important habit to develop and is useful for checking answers. This is also useful when calculators are introduced in Year 5. It is also good mathematical practice.

Table 4.3   Written calculations in Key Stage 2 for multiplication

Year 3	Year 4	Year 5	Year 6
Not applicable	TU × U	HTU × U	ThHTU × U
	Short multiplication.	TU × TU	HTU × TU
		Long multiplication	Long multiplication
		introduced. Work	continues and is
		to one decimal	refined. Work extends
		place is introduced.	to two decimal places.

The first method is the grid method (Figure 4.21). Although the National Numeracy Strategy classifies this method as informal, it is extremely efficient and tackles both long and short multiplication. This method and those in Figures 4.22–4.26 depend on the Mental Maths teaching in preceding years. To utilise these methods, children must have the opportunity to develop a series of good mental strategies. In Figure 4.22 the grid method is applied to long multiplication. The crucial awareness for both these calculations is what happens to multiples of 10 when multiplied first by units and then by other multiples of 10. Once this understanding is clear the method works extremely effectively.

Figure 4.23 demonstrates a second method of multiplication. It uses partitioning and develops into an efficient formal method using many of the skills developed in

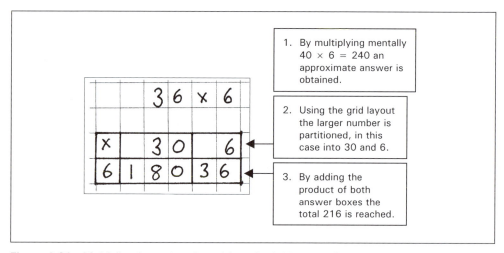

Figure 4.21   Multiplication using the grid method, Years 4–6

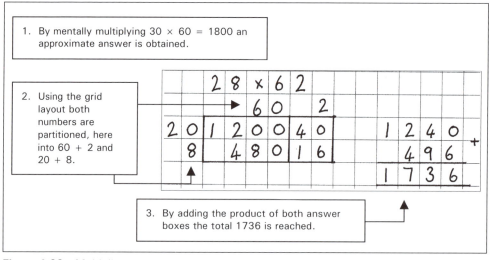

Figure 4.22   Multiplication using the grid method, Years 4–6

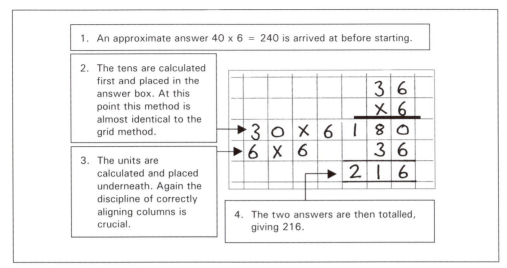

Figure 4.23 Short multiplication using partitioning, Years 4–6.

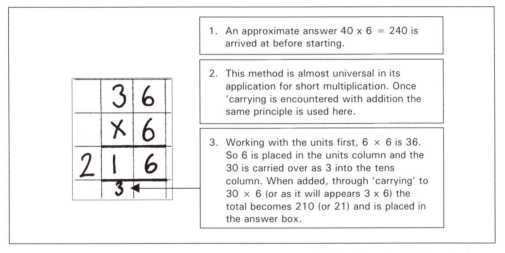

Figure 4.24 Short multiplication using partitioning, introducing 'carrying', Years 4–6.

the grid method. The method applies to both long and short multiplication. Although efficient once introduced, the formal method will not become the only means of written multiplication. As experience of larger numbers develops all methods should remain in use. In Figure 4.24 short multiplication becomes even more efficient through the introduction of 'carrying'. This is the next step towards efficient written methods.

The use of the grid method and partitioning continues as the numbers encountered become larger. Figure 4.25 is another example of the both forms of partitioning. Long multiplication with the partitioning method is possible (Figure 4.26). With development across this range of written calculation children should develop an

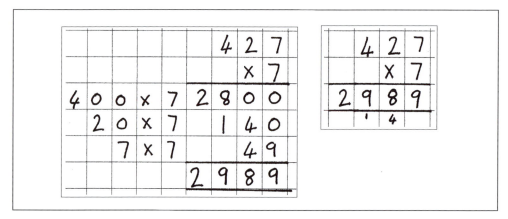

Figure 4.25 Multiplication using partitioning, Years 4–6

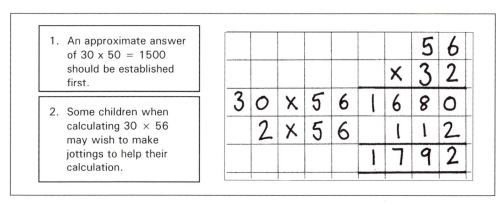

Figure 4.26 Long multiplication using partitioning, Years 4–6

understanding of the process simultaneously with written competence. Crucially it can only aid mathematical development when introduced at an appropriate stage. Other methods that can cope with these calculations do not require the dexterity of this one.

Division

As with multiplication (the inverse of division), division calculations are approximated before a written method is used. The two methods outlined in the National Numeracy Strategy rely heavily on the fact that multiplication is the inverse of division. The progression of division is identified in Table 4.4.

Adults and children can bring much negativity to discussions of division. Sound mental calculation work in division and multiplication up to Year 3 is the basis upon which the strategy builds its written methods for division and this should avoid the negativity. Good understanding of mental methods in multiplication and division is

Table 4.4   Written calculations in Key Stage 2 for division

Year 3	Year 4	Year 5	Year 6
Not applicable	TU ÷ U Should encounter remainders.	HTU ÷ U Use remainders frequently.	HTU ÷ TU Introduction of long division. Express remainders as fractions and work with decimals to two decimal places.

crucial to these methods. Two methods are used for both short and long division. The first method, using multiples of the divisor, is annotated in Figures 4.27 and 4.28. In Year 4 it has two forms. This method of using multiples continues in later year groups with larger numbers. The second method (Figure 4.28) becomes the basis upon which remaining methods that use multiples of the divisor are developed.

Short division by a standard written method (Figure 4.29) also starts in Year 4. Key skills are interchangeable between methods. Work with these methods continues into Year 5 where, as with previous developments, the calculations involve larger numbers. A contraction of the method occurs with the short division calculation when focusing upon HTU ÷ U (Figure 4.30). This method will not be the only way children are introduced to HTU ÷ U. They will encounter it first using the 'multiples of the divisor method' and also by the extended short division method. Figure 4.31 is an example of the same calculation using this method. Extensive practice with this method will ensure that when the contracted form is introduced, understanding of the process is preserved.

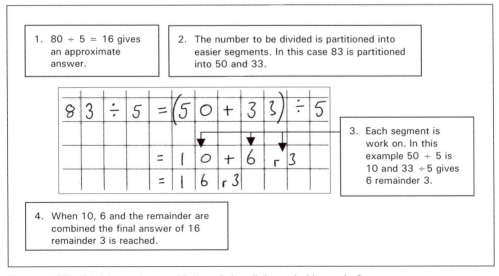

Figure 4.27   Division using multiples of the divisor, 1, Years 4–6

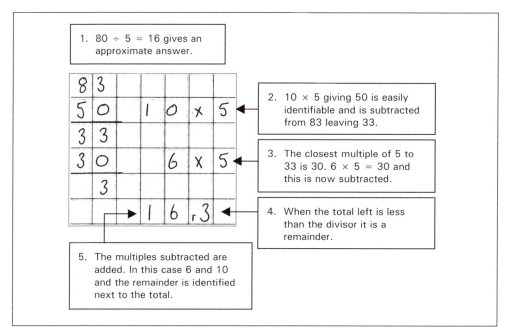

Figure 4.28   Division using multiples of the divisor, 2, Years 4–6

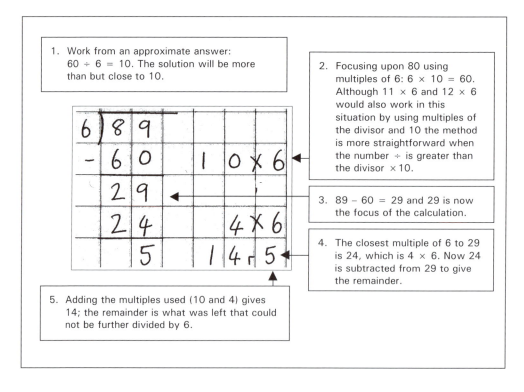

Figure 4.29   Short division with TU ÷ U, Years 4–6

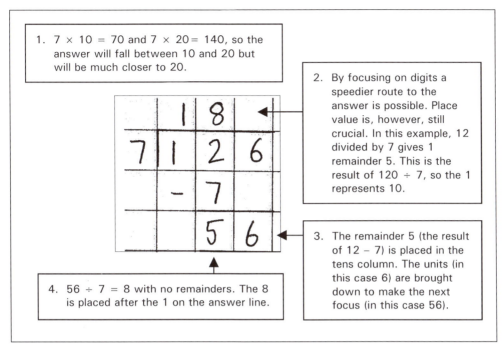

1. $7 \times 10 = 70$ and $7 \times 20 = 140$, so the answer will fall between 10 and 20 but will be much closer to 20.

2. By focusing on digits a speedier route to the answer is possible. Place value is, however, still crucial. In this example, 12 divided by 7 gives 1 remainder 5. This is the result of $120 \div 7$, so the 1 represents 10.

3. The remainder 5 (the result of $12 - 7$) is placed in the tens column. The units (in this case 6) are brought down to make the next focus (in this case 56).

4. $56 \div 7 = 8$ with no remainders. The 8 is placed after the 1 on the answer line.

Figure 4.30   Contracted short division with HTU ÷ U, Years 4–6

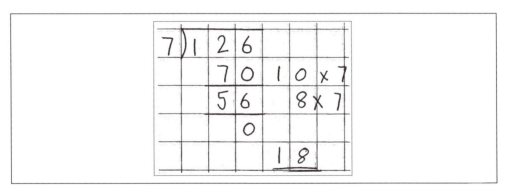

Figure 4.31   Short division with HTU ÷ U, Years 4–6

Long division is introduced in Year 6. During this time remainders become expressed as fractions. Both of these developments depend on the experience of previous years. Both methods, 'using multiples of the divisor' and 'long division', are examined here. Figure 4.32 demonstrates multiples of 10 playing the key role in both calculations. This method is efficient and straightforward. By choosing the right multiples in the calculation, negativity that can exist for long multiplication is avoided. Children may need to practise choosing multiples. In this example the number of steps can be reduced if 20×32 is used at the start. Decisions like these come through practice.

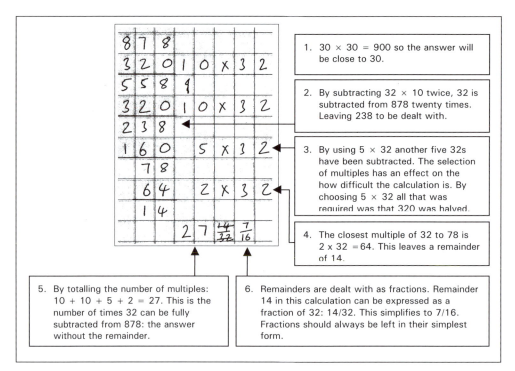

Figure 4.32   Division using multiples of the divisor, HTU ÷ TU, Years 4–6

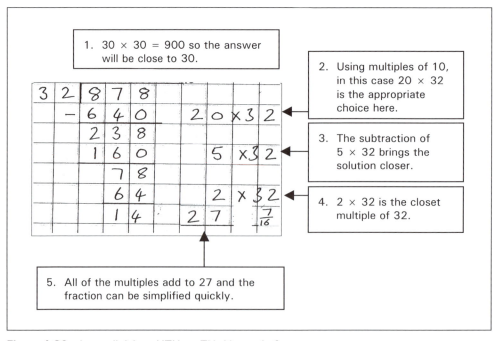

Figure 4.33   Long division, HTU ÷ TU, Years 4–6

The second method is standard for long division. In Figure 4.33 the same calculation is repeated. As with short division this calculation can also be used in a contracted form.

Conclusion

Written methods in the National Numeracy Strategy are built on effective mental calculation. If mental calculation has not developed the strategy will not meet its goal for 11-year-olds, which is that they are competent using formal methods of written calculation with a firm understanding of how methods work. Children will not learn written calculations in Key Stage 1 but their progression during the whole of Key Stage 2 depends on the mental competencies learnt in Key Stage 1. It is important that teachers and parents of children in Key Stage 1 understand that. They must also appreciate the harm that a premature introduction of formal written calculation can have on a child's mathematics. To introduce written methods before a child has developed some vital mathematical understandings, such as place value, is potentially damaging.

The effects of this often manifest themselves as children peak in mathematics. A child who has made good progress for some time mathematically stops progressing. The problem arises when the child achieves success based on either a series of misconceptions that sometimes work, or remembering rules of mathematics without the understanding to support them. This can often mean that a child's initial progress is halted (see Chapter 7).

The National Numeracy Strategy's way of tackling this and other mathematics learning issues is to promote understanding. This promotion occurs in a number of areas. Teachers will teach mathematics directly. They will be freed from many of the forces that prevented them from focusing on teaching as lengthy unmanageable assessment processes are removed and long-term planning is provided. Written methods will be taught by developing written skills in tandem with understanding. While progression in written methods will generally develop as outlined in the strategy, if the simultaneous goal of understanding and skill is to be achieved there will be times when children progress faster and slower through these methods.

CHAPTER 5

Information and communications technology and numeracy

In this chapter, we address the incorporation of computers and other technologies into the National Numeracy Strategy. The nature of learning that takes place when using technology, its organisation, resourcing and the variety of roles that technology plays in mathematics lessons are considered. The hardware and software available to support the use of information and communications technology (ICT) in numeracy lessons are outlined, and a model for software evaluation is provided.

What is ICT?

ICT in schools is generally taken to refer only to computers, but as defined by the National Numeracy Strategy it also includes: 'the calculator and extends to the whole range of audio visual aids, including audio tape, video film and educational broadcasts' (DfEE 1999c: 31). The computers available to teachers and pupils in schools vary between local authorities and between schools. The guidance in the strategy is non-specific, particular software programs are not prescribed and ICT is not linked to specific learning objectives: 'Specific programs are not mentioned, since the focus in the supplements is on mathematical outcomes, not the resources that can be used to achieve them' (DfEE 1999c: 32). This does not mean that suitable software is not available and examples, including 'Developing Number', developed by the Association of Teachers of Mathematics (ATM) specifically for numeracy, are included.

In this chapter, we divide ICT into two broad areas: computerised and non-computerised. The potential uses of equipment in both these categories are examined.

Learning with computers

Skills versus tools

Computers can play a valuable role in developing numeracy work in the classroom. Pupils respond well to using computers and are often highly motivated. Using this motivation to develop enjoyment and learning is crucial to the effective use of computers. There is, however, a distinction between learning *supported* by ICT, and the learning *of* computer skills.

The learning *of* computer skills – accessing programs, using the mouse, saving work, etc. – are important skills, which the pupils must have in order to make effective use of the computer when working independently. How these skills are taught varies, but they are different from the learning that is *supported* by computers. Learning *supported* by ICT happens when technology is used to advance the learning of a particular curriculum area or concept. We discuss the many ways in which this can be achieved in numeracy later in the chapter. The use of computers as a learning stimulus is identified in the National Numeracy Strategy. The many other potential applications such as reinforcement, teaching new skills and practice are given less attention.

Classroom organisation

Many factors can affect the learning taking place using computers, but software and classroom organisation are the most significant.

Using a computer with the whole class

Using a computer with the whole class is clearly recommended by the authors of the National Numeracy Strategy: 'When you are working directly with the whole class you need to: demonstrate and explain using a board, flip chart, computer or OHP [overhead projector]' (DfEE 1999c: 14). Unfortunately, no additional guidance is provided for this. To use a computer with the whole class effectively, the screen must be big enough to be seen by all the pupils. The smallest monitor size that makes this feasible is 17" and the pupils should be seated on the carpet in front of it. Once all the pupils can see the screen and respond to questions about the display, teaching and learning is possible. This interaction is similar to the big-book, text-level work in the literacy hour.

In order to have the whole class seated at their desks and still be able to see the display, a more radical solution is needed. A good quality large screen TV can be cheaply connected to a computer and a reasonable image produced. For schools with more money, a video projector, interactive whiteboard or liquid crystal display (LCD) overlay for an overhead projector are all powerful tools which can add significantly to this sort of work (see Appendix 2).

Using software programs with the whole class allows the discussion of a range of issues, such as graphical representations of data or equations, patterns in number, computer models, etc. A breakdown of suitable program types is provided later.

Using the computer with a small group

Working in small groups allows greater interaction with pupils. Discussion can be more focused and specifically targeted to meet the learning needs of the group. Thus each child's understanding is easier to assess and a better platform to develop learning is developed. It also makes using a smaller screen viable. A 14" monitor will allow a group of ten children seated round a group of tables a clear view of the screen. Learning develops through the complex interactions between the teacher, pupils and the computer.

Using the computer individually or in pairs

It is also possible for some pupils to use computers individually as part of numeracy lessons, although this is not recommended for all in the National Numeracy Strategy: 'Individual use of computer programs is usually inappropriate in the daily lesson, except where pupils with profound special needs or exceptional ability are doing individualised work' (DfEE 1999c: 32). It is also difficult to organise individual or paired work because of the number of groups that are to be working at any one time: 'An aim of the daily mathematics lesson is to keep the class working together and to link, but to limit to no more than three the number of different activities going on during group work' (DfEE 1999c: 31). The consequence of this is that in a class of 30 children it is not feasible to have mainstream pupils using machines (individually or even in pairs) during the numeracy lesson unless a minimum of five machines are available. This would enable a group of ten pupils to work in pairs. However, it is stated in the strategy that such work is valuable when it takes place at home, during breaks and in after school clubs. This is useful because a great deal of good software is available, which is suitable for this kind of work.

Software

As well as classroom organisation, the selection of software is crucial to learning. As the National Numeracy Strategy becomes established, software tailored to meet its learning objectives will become available. At the time of writing, the only software specifically designed to support its delivery and available for testing was the 'Developing Number Series' from the Association of Teachers of Mathematics (ATM), which is outlined in Figure 5.1. Despite the fact that little software has been designed specifically for the National Numeracy Strategy, other software is available and very useful. Tables 5.1 and 5.2 outline the major types of software available for primary school mathematics.

Developing Number Series (ATM)

This package is supplied on one 3½" disk and loads straight onto the hard disk of the computer. It is compatible with all versions of Windows from 3.1 to date. It contains three programs outlined below. The programs are all designed to allow pupils to browse through tasks and to complete exercises staged for progression. The programs are designed to suit children of all abilities and are suitable for both whole class teaching and individual work. Teachers can enter class lists and track the progress of individual pupils. The instruction booklet is comprehensive and easy to understand.

Complements
Helps students develop the ability to find complements to 10, 20, ..., 100 (and the decimal equivalents – e.g. complements to 0.1, 0.2, ... 1.0). The program differs from basic drill and practice in that it uses the image of a 100 square to help pupils develop flexible mental arithmetic strategies, e.g. becoming aware that if they can calculate 10 – 4 they can also calculate 30 – 24, 70 – 64, and so on.

Numbers
Helps pupils learn to read, write and say numbers, and to recognise the place value of individual digits. The range of digits to be worked on can be varied from 1–99, 1–9,999,999, 0.001–999, and so on. This helps pupils develop an understanding of place value and gain confidence when working with very large numbers. The diagram below shows some of the links that parents, teachers and pupils can draw from the numbers program.

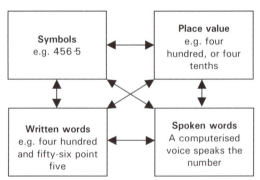

Tables
Helps pupils develop the mental strategies to work out their multiplication tables using only the following: double, halve, multiply by 10, add on or take away one number (except for 7 × 7 = 49). These strategies are displayed on the screen, along with a number grid in the basic levels. Progression is catered for, with tasks of increasing complexity and the addition of time pressures.

Figure 5.1 The Developing Number Series software (program descriptions and numbers diagram adapted from ATM (1999))

Table 5.1 Office style software

Software	Summary of use	Examples
Spreadsheets	Essentially a collection of boxes (cells) that can carry out calculations. The information from one cell can be linked to others to allow one result to affect another. Useful for data handling activities, simple surveys and graph work of all types.	Microsoft Excel, Number Box
Databases	Based on old-style card files, these programs allow users to store large amounts of information about lots of different things. In mathematics they can be used to allow large numbers of records to be compared with respect to certain attributes (fields). They are good for enabling pupils to work with large survey numbers.	Microsoft Access First Workshop Information Workshop Data Explorer

Table 5.2 Educational software

Software	Summary of use	Examples
Question generators	These programs are also termed 'drill and practice'. Questions of various styles (depending on the program) are shown on the screen and the pupils input the answer.	Hooray for Henrietta Megamaths Tables
Pattern generators	The computer generates a number grid, line or sequence and the pupils search for patterns to derive the answer.	Monty Number Snake Number Grids
Movement control	These programs are usually based on LOGO and require the pupils to control the movement on screen of an object, often through mazes. They can also be used to help pupils generate pictures.	Logotron Software LOGO NRICH website (Figure 5.5)
Puzzles	Often based on traditional logic games such as 'Frogs' and Noughts and Crosses.	Microsmile Maths Software Puzzles
Investigations	Computer controlled mathematical investigations, pupils must use the information given and their mathematical knowledge to solve the problems or generate their own explanations.	Websites (Figure 5.5) Granada Breakaway Maths
Simulations	These programs simulate a range of activities from flight to managing a shop or football team.	CSH Cars; Maths in Motion; Maths Explorer

Discussion is key to the learning of mathematics, as is the questioning process facilitated by the teacher or group leader (see Chapter 3). The types of software available are discussed further below and where appropriate good starting points for numeracy lessons and other computer mathematics are included. How any software is used with a class is a matter of professional judgement. However, when used with a whole class or group, the teacher can use a range of questions to promote discussion and this process is generally more important for the learning process than the software being used. Appendix 3 gives titles and distributors for software under the headings used below.

Spreadsheets

Spreadsheets are hugely flexible and powerful tools for mathematics teachers and although new users may initially find them daunting, they are quickly mastered and rewarding to use. Some educational spreadsheets (such as 'Number Box') come preloaded with templates which allow pupils and teachers to carry out activities quickly without having to deal with complex formulas. They can be used for everything from modelling the repeated roll of dice to recording the growth of a plant.

The teaching of 'function machines' can be aided through spreadsheets. A formula can be allocated to a cell and deleted if required. This means that numbers can be 'input' and the 'machine's output' displayed. The teacher can then encourage discussion about what the function could be and help pupils test the effect of changing the function on the output.

Spreadsheets are also powerful tools for drawing graphs quickly. This can extend function machine work by allowing graphs of functions to be displayed quickly and is also useful for aspects of data handling. For example the teacher can quickly produce a graph of 'ice-cream sales' and the class can discuss what is being shown and model how it might change with the weather. The power of using the computer is that these changes can be illustrated at the touch of a button.

Databases

Like spreadsheets, databases can seem daunting and difficult to use effectively. This is less true with school versions, which are simplified and often include templates for standard tasks. Databases are very powerful tools for the teaching of data handling. They are particularly good when carrying out large surveys covering lots of information about a class, or information about a whole-school population. They allow the class or group to look for links between more than one variable, e.g. 'Do tall people all have large feet?' or 'Is it only blond people who have blue eyes?'

Question generators

The effectiveness of any question generating program depends on how well it has been set up. The National Numeracy Strategy warns: 'repetitive practice of number bonds already mastered, is not good use of lesson time' (DfEE 1999c: 32). Used outside lessons by individuals, they allow pupils to develop a quick recall of facts. The fact that the work is on the computer and often colourful provides a good stimulus and incentive to do well. This motivation helps ensure that effective learning takes place.

The use of these programs by pairs of pupils is even more valuable. Placing questions on the wall by the computer such as 'How did you do that?', 'Is there a quicker way of doing that?', etc. gives pupils the vocabulary to talk about their work. This means that mental strategies will be refined more effectively than by individual use.

Pattern generators

These programs are excellent for use as a class, group or individual stimulus. They are used in a similar way to discussing looking for patterns in a 100 square, but the sequence of numbers displayed can be changed. This means that emphasis on particular tables is possible. Animation makes them more enjoyable for pupils than posters and therefore increases motivation and learning.

Movement and control

'Logo' is a basic programming language. Computer programs and computerised robots like 'Roamer' and 'Pip' (see Appendix 2) which enable pupils to use LOGO are valuable because of the skills they promote. Pupils develop problem-solving skills by breaking down complex tasks into a series of smaller steps. Logical thinking, skills of estimation and discussion can all be developed through simple LOGO activities. Suitable activities include moving the robot or screen turtle from a starting point to a target area in as few moves as possible. The initial attempt can then be refined through discussion or trial and error and more efficient methods found. Figure 5.2 shows a creative approach to using LOGO.

Ask the group to tell you a popular story. A good one for this purpose is Goldilocks and the Three Bears. Different versions abound and there is much interest in agreeing a version. Was the porridge too hot, too salty or too sweet? Why did she reject all the chairs except baby bears, etc.? This is a good, but not particularly mathematical discussion to have.

Once this discussion has been completed and a version debated a task can be set. Ask the group to select a scene from the story and draw a picture of it using LOGO. This is open ended in that the class select what to draw, but mathematically sound because to draw the scene they will be using key mathematical principles: orientating the turtle with angle; using calculation to complete any window frames or chairs they draw; and developing their estimation skills when they consider how large to make objects. Erasing is also often highly mathematical, requiring an exact retracing of steps.

If you have only one computer it is at this point that others in the group could design their scene on paper. At this point you need to stress the limitations of LOGO as a draw package. This task is concerned with developing children's use of mathematics to portray a picture rather than ICT to develop art.

Figure 5.2 A semi-structured LOGO activity (Fraser 2000)

Puzzles

These programs are generally games that develop logic. The activities used will depend on the games being played. In general they are best suited for use by pairs or small groups of pupils. They can also be used for introducing a particular mathematics game to the whole class that they will then play on paper or using a board (e.g. 'Othello', 'Nimb'; see Chapter 6). Such games can help pupils improve concentration, look for patterns and develop problem-solving strategies. Using a computer to play the games has the advantage that there is less opportunity for arguments over the rules and the teacher can more closely manage the learning.

Investigations

These programs have a big overlap with puzzles but have a wider scope. Adventure games can reveal a little information early on, and then, as the pupils require help, progressively more information, which has to be pieced together to reach a solution. At a more basic level, simple investigations can be set up so clues are given when pupils are stuck. Potential also exists for investigations to be collaborative through use of the Internet and email. This sort of work is most suitable for groups of children to establish collaboration and discussion. The cross-curricular use of mathematics in solving problems in ICT and other subjects is also discussed in the National Numeracy Strategy (DfEE 1999c: 17).

Simulations

These programs give a real-life scenario or an illustration of the practical uses of mathematics. The activities chosen will depend on what is being simulated. Whether navigating a ship, building a new civilisation or running a cafe, the situation can motivate pupils. The pupils apply their knowledge of mathematics to a 'realistic' situation. This helps them to stop relying on standard methods, to combine more than one operation and draw together different concepts.

Evaluating software

Having decided on the type of software it is important to evaluate the usefulness of specific programs on offer. Most companies will now allow schools to have an evaluation copy of their programs so they can 'try before they buy'. This is a time-consuming process, but it can prevent costly, frustrating mistakes. The reason that this is so important is that although a program can be very well intentioned it often displays simple problems that greatly reduce its usefulness in the classroom. There are also important issues relating to how the software is designed. Figure 5.3 provides

- Name of program?

- Does it fully install or run from CD?
  This is important because with some software, even when a school has purchased a site licence, they still need to purchase additional CDs if the software is to be used in more than one computer at a time. Additionally, CDs are easily damaged. If the software can be installed and run from the hard disk, this problem is easier to prevent.

- Is it compatible with all the versions of Windows/Mac OS/Archimedes RISC OS in use in school? Do you have enough memory and hard disk space? And if you update your computers will the program still be of use?
  This is simply a question of flexibility. If all the computers in school are the same then it may not pose a problem. The same is true within year groups. The problems can arise if for example, some Year 5 classes have Windows 95 machines and others have Windows 98 machines and the software will only run on one of them. This makes planning the use of the program across the year group difficult.

- What ICT skills are required before the mathematical learning can take place?
  This goes back to the difference between the learning of computer skills compared to learning supported by ICT. If the program is difficult to load or requires high-level mouse or keyboard skills, the computer can be a barrier to the learning for some children. Of course, it will eventually help children develop their ICT skills, but during this period it is not mathematics skills that are being learnt.

- On loading are the instructions clear?
  Will most children be able to use the program effectively without repeated support from the teacher (for non-mathematical reasons). This is particularly important if the program is likely to be used by children working independently.

- Will it be used with the whole class, small groups or individuals?
  It is important to understand this in order to assess its usefulness in the classroom, and also because the significance of the other questions above is reduced if most of the ICT issues are to be dealt with by the teacher.

- Can the teacher set the level for individual pupils?
  This is important because, if not, the pupil can spend their 20 minutes of computer time working at a basic level and not actually learn very much. If the level can be set, the pupil can use that time more effectively. Also, is it made clear to the teacher what is covered in each level? This is vital to prevent the teacher having to work through all the levels in order to establish which will be suitable for each group within the class.

Figure 5.3   Teacher software evaluation sheet

- Does it remember individual pupils or to they have to start again from the beginning every time?
  This relates simply to the wasted time for pupils and teachers in setting up the program, choosing levels and progressing to the point at which they finished the previous time they used the computer.

- Does the teacher receive feedback about each pupil's performance?
  If the pupils are working independently, it is useful for the teacher to be able to check their performance. A great deal of information is found in pupils' incorrect responses and if the computer stores these, learning can be advanced by allowing the teacher to analyse them.

- Can you add your own questions?
  This feature makes it possible to tailor the program to suit individual pupils and to ensure that it relates directly to the work being covered in class. For example, if a class has been using doubling and near doubles for mental calculations, then the program could be tailored to support this.

- Does it meet a large number of learning objectives or is it very specific?
  Clearly this relates to whether or not the software will be useful across a range of abilities, ages and curriculum areas. If it is not then it may still be useful to a school, but an understanding of its classroom use is necessary to make a value for money judgement.

- What happens when the pupils give an incorrect answer?
  This is particularly important because of the new ways of working for pupils, which the National Numeracy Strategy seeks to encourage. For example, some mathematics software will lead pupils down a route to a standard calculation (e.g. vertical tens and units addition) when they make an incorrect response, which might be inappropriate to the learning occurring through the strategy.

- Does it encourage creative thinking or simply reinforce standard calculations?
  This is partly a question of investigation versus drill and practice. Both sorts of programs have a place, but it is important to be aware of the learning that is taking place. It is important because a program that is encouraging pupils to carry out complex calculations may not reflect the way in which a pupil is calculating the answer. For example some programs are designed to accept answers only in a specific format – e.g. units first – which may be counter-intuitive to a pupil's own method.

Figure 5.3   Teacher software evaluation sheet (continued)

a list of some of the areas to consider when purchasing software, in the form of a question sheet for teachers to work through.

Busy teachers may not have time to complete this process thoroughly, but older and more able children are good 'testers' of software. They are particularly useful because they will soon find any 'holes' that may exist in a program, which teachers may miss. For this reason a pro forma for pupils is also included (Figure 5.4).

- What is your name?
- What is the program you are using?
- Did you load it yourself or did you get help?
- Did you find the instructions easy to understand (circle one)?
    - Easy   OK   Hard   No instructions
- Was the program: (circle one)
    - Fun   OK   Boring
- Why?
- Did it go wrong when you were using it (circle one)?
    - Yes   No
- What would you change about it?
- Was it too hard, too easy or just right?
- Would you like to use it again?

Figure 5.4 Pupil software evaluation sheet

Teachers' use of computers

The computer is an important tool for teachers as well as for pupils. The Internet can provide access to a wealth of ideas, particularly for investigations which pupils can carry out. The National Numeracy Strategy document points out that the websites of the mathematical associations are useful in this area and for providing links to other related websites. As the National Grid for Learning develops it should allow teachers to support each other by sharing planning and ideas for the teaching of mathematics and other subjects. The Internet can also provide email facilities which teachers could use with their class to support mathematical projects, linking their pupils with those in other schools both in this country and abroad. Figure 5.5 shows some useful websites that provide a good starting point for parents and teachers looking to improve their pupils enjoyment of numeracy.

Additionally, a spreadsheet program such as 'Microsoft Excel' can allow teachers to store the marks of their pupils electronically and reproduce these in different formats, allowing them to monitor their pupils' performance closely. The results for a particular pupil over a period of time can be presented graphically, allowing them to be discussed easily with the pupil and enabling formulation of a strategy to further improve their performance.

Websites are prone to change particularly those that are home pages of individuals and small organisations. The addresses included here should be reliable, and up-to-date links can be found from them.

http://members.aol.com/garethhon/
The home page of the authors contains links to the sites listed below and others as they become available, along with details of the authors and their research interests.

www.nrich.Maths.org.uk
This is probably the best mathematics site on the web. The National Royal Institution Cambridge Homerton (NRICH) online mathematics club offers free newsletters for children, lots of problem-solving activities with children's solutions posted on the Web, games, a question answering service, LOGO and much more.

www.bbc.co.uk
This is the home page of BBC television and radio. This site is obviously not dedicated to mathematics, but it does provide many useful links to up-to-date mathematics sites, aimed at parents, teachers and children.

www.anglia.co.uk/education/Mathsnet/
Aimed primarily at secondary school pupils and teachers, this site contains some material that is of use to upper primary teachers. As well as daily facts and puzzles, investigations and links to other sites, downloadable Microsoft Excel (spreadsheet) templates are available. A program which displays animated three-dimensional shapes will also be very useful in the classroom as a stimulus.

www.soton.ac.uk/gary/crime.html
This is the home page for the Centre for Research in Maths Education (CRIME) at Southampton University. It is useful for keeping up-to-date with current developments in mathematics education and has useful links to other mathematics sites.

Figure 5.5   Some useful websites

Using computers to support pupils with special educational needs (SEN)

The area of differentiation is clearly seen as a suitable application of ICT in the National Numeracy Strategy. In discussing how to cater for pupils who are very able, the following suggestions are made: 'They can be stretched through ... extra challenges – including investigations using ICT' (DfEE 1999c: 20). The strategy states that SEN support is an appropriate use of computers for individual members of the class. Drill and practice programs and integrated learning systems could well support the learning of the least able. The strategy does highlight the danger of using 'endless practice of number bonds already mastered' (DfEE 1999c: 32) and this is something that one needs to be aware of when setting up these programs.

The use of non-computerised equipment

Overhead projectors

Until the arrival of the national numeracy and literacy hours the OHP's use in primary schools was limited. OHPs can be used to make many printed resources visible for all the pupils in a class. In order to be effective the classroom requires blackout facilities and a suitable screen, unless a high powered, modern and expensive model is purchased. Some schools use a whiteboard as a screen, but these may be too reflective. Simple ideas such as using a 100 square projected on to the wall allows the teacher to discuss patterns in number with the class. The teacher can use coloured pens to mark these to make them clearer. This work can be extended by blanking numbers out, possibly with a number cross (see Figure 5.6). This sort of

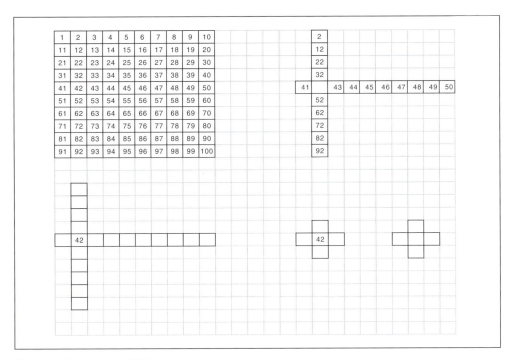

Figure 5.6 Using a 100 square and number cross

activity can be used for modelling work children will go through themselves during the group aspect of the lesson. If used with an overlay, the OHP can also enable the class to view computerised ICT resources, such as demonstration calculators and computer screens: 'For example, you could use an overhead projector calculator for whole-class demonstration purposes' (DfEE 1999c: 8).

Tape recorders

Tape recorders are so common in primary schools that few people would consider them to be an ICT resource and their usefulness is often overlooked. There are many simple possibilities for their use. For example, pupils who have weak reading skills due to their age, a specific learning difficulty or because English is an additional language for them, can have spoken instructions for their tasks, enabling greater independence during the group work activity. Tape recorders can be used with the whole class for table songs and nursery rhymes, which can assist pupils' understanding of counting. Pupils can also use a tape recorder to record the results of investigations, which both aids independence and promotes use of mathematical language.

Video

Commercially produced pre-recorded tapes and broadcasts recorded by the school can provide a stimulus for mathematics work, in a similar way to computers, especially on shape and space, tessellation and other very visual areas. They can also provide a useful starting point for investigations. For video use to be effective it must be used appropriately. The material chosen should be relevant to the area being studied and appeal to the pupils using it. As indicated earlier in this chapter and in Chapters 2 and 3, discussion is a key feature of mathematical learning and appropriate questioning is crucial. If a good quality video recorder and cassette are used then the teacher can freeze the image and allow the class to ask questions about it and discuss their views.

The availability of a video camera extends the possibilities further. This allows the teacher to record instructions and the pupils to record the results of their work, especially investigations. These are similar uses to those of audio tape recorders, but the results can be even more rewarding.

Conclusions

ICT in the broad sense can be a valuable teaching tool for delivering aspects of the National Numeracy Strategy. It can be used to illustrate difficult concepts, support learning by assisting pupils to develop their own mental strategies and make learning more fun. If ICT can enhance the learning process by making concepts clearer to pupils or providing motivation and increased enjoyment then it should be used. However, ICT should be used carefully. Teachers or parents should carefully evaluate what they are trying to achieve and plan carefully how ICT can support this. It is only through careful preparation, planning and resourcing that ICT will improve pupils' learning. Simply putting a pupil in front of a computer screen will not guarantee learning.

CHAPTER 6

Mathematics investigations

In this chapter we examine mathematics investigations in detail and explore the benefits to pupils and parents. We address the different categories of investigations and the roles they can play, along with how to choose those most appropriate. We include examples of investigations of different types to give a context for the discussion of the learning they promote and to give parents and teachers a starting point for integrating them into their teaching.

What are mathematics investigations?

Mathematics investigations are mathematical activities which, although structured, are also open-ended. They can take the form of challenges or problems to solve and generally differ from 'normal' classroom mathematics. They vary in context, content and style, but have the common link of developing pupils' investigative skills. Investigations reinforce the idea that standard methods are less important than the thought process and the application of knowledge. They depend on pupils using their mathematical knowledge in different situations, listening to others and revisiting the problem in different ways. These skills are useful, both in everyday life and in Standard Assessment Tasks (SATs) exams. Mathematics investigations also form a compulsory part of GCSE mathematics courses.

What can be achieved through mathematics investigations?

When used appropriately, mathematics investigations create a host of opportunities for parents, teachers and pupils. For example, they can:

- give a real life context to mathematics problems;
- improve logical thought processes;

- build teamwork;
- encourage use and application of number;
- develop problem-solving skills;
- stretch the more able;
- support the less able;
- improve spatial awareness;
- raise the status of mathematics;
- motivate pupils; and
- make mathematics more fun!

The place of investigations in the National Numeracy Strategy

Investigations are very important tools for the mathematics teacher. They can develop a huge range of skills, but their use is not explicit in the National Numeracy Strategy apart from to extend more able pupils:

> The yearly teaching programs described in the framework leave about one week in each term unallocated, when pupils who are very able can, for example, carry out a sustained mathematical investigation and continue it at home. There are many good publications to support this kind of work and schools with access to the Internet can also download suitable material from a problem solving website. (DfEE 1999c: 21)

Despite this initial impression, the authors of the National Numeracy Strategy clearly do view investigations as important. The strategy's five-day course discusses problem solving at some length. The DfEE publication *Reasoning about Numbers, with Challenges and Simplifications* includes examples of investigations. These should:

> help children to:
> - solve mathematical problems or puzzles, recognise and explain patterns and relationships, generalise and predict;
> - explain methods and reasoning orally and in writing;
> - suggest extensions by asking ' What if …?' (DfEE 1999b: 1)

Choosing suitable investigations

Having established the value of investigations we now explore using them with a class. Investigations are about as numerous and varied as the pupils in a class. They span every area of the mathematics curriculum and cross ability levels. Having decided to carry out a mathematics investigation with your class, either regularly or as a 'one-off', it is important to decide what you want to achieve through it, and to choose an appropriate investigation to target these aims. Many aims can be met with most investigations, if planned correctly (e.g. teamwork), while others require more specific investigations (e.g. spatial awareness). The aims of investigations outlined in the strategy and associated publications are very much related to specific mathematical outcomes. Although we agree that these are important, so are the areas we outlined at the beginning of this chapter – making mathematics more fun, raising its status, etc. – and when choosing an investigation these are valid and important areas to consider.

To assist with the process of choosing an investigation, we have included examples that have been used effectively with classes. For each we have outlined how it could be used in school and the skills that it develops.

The investigations

Unifix towers investigation

This investigation (Figure 6.1) is accessible to pupils at different levels. For most pupils it begins as a construction exercise, looking at extending a sequence or pattern. For younger or weaker pupils it will remain at this level and is valuable. For more able or experienced pupils it forms the beginnings of algebra, understanding a numerical progression, developing an understandable means of recording (notation) and extending the sequence mathematically. From this stage the pupils can generalise a rule which can predict the number of cubes for any position in the sequence (nth terms).

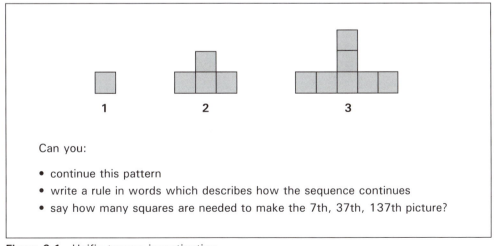

Can you:

- continue this pattern
- write a rule in words which describes how the sequence continues
- say how many squares are needed to make the 7th, 37th, 137th picture?

Figure 6.1 Unifix towers investigation

The activity encourages pupils to discuss what they are seeing and to predict what happens later in the sequence. They should also be encouraged to solve the problem in their own way. This will help their understanding that several methods can be successful and that certain methods will be more efficient and more appropriate to the problem.

This activity is best suited to pupils working in pairs or possibly small groups. At a basic level it could extend over two sessions. Further lessons could involve modelling further sequences.

Crossing rivers investigations

These types of investigations (Figure 6.2) are useful for developing logical thought processes in pupils. They are generally enjoyed by pupils and can provide excellent motivation as they are seen as different to 'normal maths'. They help pupils develop recording strategies and can allow them to use materials as well as pencil and paper to attempt solutions. They can also be acted out, which is reassuring to pupils with reading and comprehension difficulties or those who lack confidence.

Both activities could be carried out by a whole class, groups, pairs or individual pupils. As a whole-class activity, modelling by members of the class enables all pupils to take part at some level. If this is not carried out then it is most appropriate for more able pupils. One session for the activity is appropriate, with further work at home if required. Carrying out both activities at close intervals would usually be inappropriate.

Two adults and two children want to cross a river. They have a canoe that can carry two children or one adult. Any one of them can paddle the canoe. What is the shortest number of journeys in which they can all cross the river?	A farmer needs to cross a river. She has a canoe that can carry her and two objects across the river. Unfortunately she has to move a fox, a chicken and some grain. If left alone together, or confined in the canoe, the chicken will eat the grain and the fox will eat the chicken. What is the shortest number of journeys in which she can take them all across the river?

Figure 6.2 Crossing rivers investigations

Milk crate investigation

This is a wonderful hands-on investigation. It can be introduced with a real milk crate and bottles or modelled using a grid and counters or on paper (Figure 6.3). It is gripping for many pupils, holding their attention for long periods of time, and is often returned to later by the pupils independently if they are not initially successful.

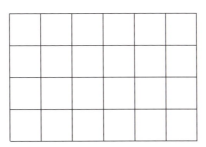

A milk crate like the one shown here holds 24 bottles.

- Is it possible to arrange 18 bottles of milk so that each row and column contains an even number of bottles?

- Is there only one way to do this?

Figure 6.3 Milk crate investigation

Discussion is promoted during work on the activity, from pupils spotting errors in each other's solutions, to sharing of successful solutions to see if they are different from each other. The other main strength of this activity is that logical thinking is encouraged, with pupils making small changes, reviewing the effect and then continuing or back-tracking. It also highlights the importance of careful recording.

'How many?' investigations

These investigations (Figure 6.4) are incredibly useful with pupils across a range of abilities. They can be differentiated easily by varying both the size of the object and the size of the space to be filled. They meet learning objectives related to shape and space, area and volume and measure. They can also give pupils experience of working with very large numbers in a real-life situation. This can help pupils develop skills in estimating and in using calculators or computers to carry out calculations involving large numbers.

This activity could extend over several sessions and is likely to require teacher guidance with all but the most able pupils. Group working will allow differentiation;

- How many pound coins would it take to fill a shoe box?

- How many pound coins would it take to fill the classroom, the hall, etc.?

- What difference would it make it you used Smarties instead of pound coins?

- What about if you used Giant Smarties or mini ones?

Figure 6.4 'How many?' investigations

less able groups can work with smaller areas and larger objects. It would also be suitable as an extension project for one or two more able pupils.

Packaging investigations

These investigations (Figure 6.5) develop pupils' understanding of volume and area, as well as nets and three-dimensional shapes. The pupils will also develop measuring skills and carry out calculations involving several shapes and combining operations. They can use their imagination to solve the problems in many different ways and also present their findings in imaginative ways.

This activity is most suitable for completion in pairs or by individuals, because disagreements over construction can mar the mathematics with larger groups. Some mixed ability groups with strong guidance will also find the activity rewarding.

Your task is to design a product to match the design brief given. You must design a mock-up from card to show your idea, which should be completed to the best of your ability given the resources available.

- **Design brief 1**
  Design a set of three suitcases. The smallest case should be half the size of the middle case and the largest should be twice the size of the middle case. The design of the cases should reflect who they are for: children, executives, travellers, etc.

- **Design brief 2**
  A cereal manufacturer has designed a new range of dehydrated breakfast cereal. It is unique in that it takes up much less volume than normal cereals because it expands only when mixed with water or milk. The box must hold exactly 100 grams of cereal when full and 24 cm^3 of the cereal weighs exactly 100 grams. Design the packaging.

Figure 6.5 Packaging investigations

Real-life contexts investigations

These investigations (Figure 6.6) have a context, which is appealing to pupils because of its real-life situation. Pupils who fail to 'see the point' of classroom mathematics often find them appealing and apply themselves well. The activities require pupils to apply their knowledge to count 'how many' of each item is required. They must then research to find the unit costs and calculate the exact cost. The activity can also be tailored to refine the skill of estimating.

This activity can be used with small groups, individuals or pairs of pupils. If required the task can be subdivided to involve the whole class and to aid differentiation. It also lends itself well to the use of calculators and computer spreadsheets, which add interest and can aid differentiation.

- As an end of term treat, the class are to be allowed to have a picnic in the school playground. Plan a list of food which everyone will have, including a drink, some savoury dishes and some sweets. You will need to work within the budget set by your class teacher and remember to include your teacher and other adults visiting when you work out your numbers.

- For insurance reasons we have to work out the total replacement cost for the equipment in the classroom. This includes all the furniture, and all the stationery such as paper and pencils, right down to the paper clips. In your groups, calculate the replacement costs of the equipment on your list and we will look at the total cost during the plenary session.

Figure 6.6 Real-life context investigations

Mathematical frogs investigation

This investigation (Figure 6.7) is always popular with pupils, particularly when it is modelled using pupils on chairs or large paper lily pads. It is valuable both because it is enjoyable and because it helps pupil focus on making small logical steps. Once again the importance of recording moves is highlighted so that pupils can replicate their results and explain their reasoning. It can easily be simplified or extended by altering the numbers of frogs and pads involved.

These mathematical frogs are frustrated. Both the red frogs (R) and the green frogs (G) want to swap sides. They can only move along the lily pads by sliding (moving along one place to an empty pad) or hopping (jumping over an occupied pad to an empty one). (Simplification: use four frogs and five lily pads.)

- What is the least number of moves this can be done in?
- Can you do this with no backward moves?
- What if there were two more pads?
- Can you find a rule that links the number of pads to the number of moves?

Figure 6.7 Mathematical frogs investigation

Nimb

Nimb is an age-old game and is captivating for most people (Figure 6.8). It can be played after very little introduction but takes a long time to master. It develops skills of analysis and problem solving. Players must make careful observations of their strategies and those of their opponents in order to refine and improve their ideas. As

 This is a game for two players. Players take turns to remove lines. They can remove as many as they want from any row, but only from one row during each turn. The loser is the player to remove the last line.

 The lines can be marked on paper or a blackboard, or counters can be used. Apparently this game was played by ancient Egyptians with piles of camel dung, which were kicked away as the game progressed.

- Can you find any patterns that always allow you to win?
- Does it matter who goes first?
- What is the smallest number of moves in which you can win? Or lose?

Figure 6.8   Nimb

pupils develop winning strategies they will learn about symmetry and number sequences, and discuss these with other pupils.

Using investigations successfully

As these examples illustrate, investigations are hugely valuable tools for teaching mathematics. They can develop a huge range of skills and have positive effects on the status of mathematics and the attitudes of pupils, but to be effective, they must be used appropriately. As a parent or teacher the process of evaluating your aims, and what can be achieved through a particular investigation, is crucial to ensure that these are compatible. A simple aim, such as raising the status of mathematics, or making mathematics lessons more enjoyable is occasionally appropriate, but when investigations are used on a regular or long-term basis, aims need to be targeted to meet specific curriculum objectives. It is also useful to provide investigations and games for pupils who are working independently, to use when they have finished their other work.

Teaching problem-solving skills

To understand the processes involved when tackling a particular investigation it is important for the teachers to carry out the activity themselves. This can be time consuming but is invaluable in order to be able to teach pupils how to approach it. Despite this preparation by the teacher, some pupils will use a different method. This should be allowed and, with guidance and support, may prove effective. This chance to explore methods is important but needs careful management to avoid pupil frustration. The unpredictability of pupils' approaches requires teachers to have a thorough grasp of the problem and its solutions before using an investigation.

Problem-solving skills are often seen as 'caught not taught', but this should not be the case. Children should be taught problem-solving skills from an early age. The following points list some of the ways in which teachers can help pupils develop their problem-solving skills:

- give practice completing investigations at an appropriate level;
- provide model solutions and thought processes for specific investigations;
- encourage discussion of strategies;
- use focused questions;
- gradually divulge more information to maintain interest;
- allow time for work on investigations to develop;
- allow pupils access to computerised investigations software; and
- encourage pupils to design their own investigations.

These will help pupils to develop the skills needed to approach problems from a position of strength. They will become used to examining the information available to them and will have access to a range of strategies with which to attempt to find solutions to problems.

Homework

Homework is now a huge focus in schools with legal requirements concerning how much should be set. This can create a huge marking burden for teachers but investigations can help alleviate this. Not all homework has to be written or valuable in its own right. The strategy states that:

you can equally well ask your class to:
- do an activity, which makes use of the home context;
- play a number game or work on a number puzzle;
- gather information to use in the next lesson: for example, collect data or take measurements;
- think about how they might solve a problem;
- prepare their contribution to a group presentation to the class.

(DfEE 1999c: 16)

Further, it comments: 'Out of class activities need to be frequent, short and focused. They should be varied, interesting and fun so that they motivate children, stimulate their learning and foster different study skills' (DfEE 1999c: 16).

Clearly, investigations are suitable activities for homework. They are enjoyable and allow pupils the opportunity to develop and practise a range of mathematical skills. The activities could be introduced to class during the plenary session and then strategies and solutions discussed at the beginning or end of the next lesson.

Despite the potential benefits of using investigations as homework activities, there are potential problems. Some investigations can require a lengthy explanation and some pupils will require more help than others. Additionally, investigations require time to be spent on them before they can be solved. This is often incompatible with pupils spending only half an hour per night on homework. It is possible to overcome this by asking pupils to spend half an hour thinking about the problem and to share what they have found out in the next lesson. Pupils are in this way not put under pressure to find the solution, but encouraged to share the strategies they have tried. Some pupils will, of course, continue to work on the activity until they have found a solution.

Another problem is that parents may not understand what the teacher is trying to achieve when investigations are not regularly used in school.

Problems introducing investigations to parents

Mathematics investigations are enjoyed by pupils and meet a wide range of objectives, but they are not always popular with parents. This is often because parents don't understand the purpose of investigations. The mathematical content of many investigations is not immediately apparent, particularly with logic games like Nimb, so parents can feel that their child is not 'being taught properly', as examined in Chapter 8. This can be prevented through communication with parents, which enables them to understand the purpose of investigations. The figures and discussion in Chapter 8 can assist with this process.

Conclusions

The National Numeracy Strategy says that: 'Your daily mathematics lessons should provide opportunities for children to practise and consolidate their skills and knowledge, to develop and extend their techniques and strategies, and to prepare for their future learning' (DfEE 1999c: 15). Maths investigations provide great opportunities for parents, pupils and teachers to enjoy numeracy. They can harness attention, help pupils develop new working relationships, promote discussion and refine skills in ways that few other activities can. They must be planned carefully and included in the school mathematics curriculum, rather than used simply as fillers or novelty activities with no clear mathematical objectives. The skills that the pupils require do not develop overnight but must be taught and nurtured. When they are, the results are always worthwhile.

CHAPTER 7

Dealing with 'sum stress'

Virtually everyone has at some point experienced extreme anxiety about some aspect of their life: job interviews, pressure at work, health, professional exams, etc. School causes pupils concern as well. 'Many students when reflecting on their time at school have reported that strong emotions were aroused by their classroom experiences, and that these greatly influenced their learning for better or worse' (Skemp 1989: 189). Concerns about school are perfectly normal and understandable, but for some pupils they can become more extreme and cause them serious problems. In this chapter we examine the effect on pupils of extreme anxiety about mathematics ('sum stress'), how it is caused and possible solutions. We look at how the National Numeracy Strategy could affect 'sum stress' sufferers. Our aim is to help children enjoy numeracy by enabling teachers and parents to remove barriers to learning.

Very little has been published on the effects of anxiety on performance in mathematics, except by Richard Skemp, Emeritus Professor at the University of Warwick. This chapter owes a great deal to his work on the psychology of learning mathematics. We have attempted to condense the key points of his highly academic texts to make them more accessible to busy teachers and parents.

What is 'sum stress'?

'Sum stress' refers to the symptoms some pupils suffer when faced with mathematical problems or even just the prospect of a mathematics lesson. Such feelings can manifest themselves in many ways. Pupils may become upset or unusually loud, or present behavioural problems. Their work in mathematics, particularly when approaching new areas of work or returning to difficult concepts may be below the standard they reach in other subjects. They may never enjoy mathematics and it may become a source of fear. Whether 'sum stress' results in a lack of success or 'just' becomes a barrier to children's enjoyment of numeracy, it needs to be addressed quickly. It is our view that 'sum stress', if not addressed, can quickly become a major barrier to learning. The following quotes from pupils we have worked with illustrate just how stressful pupils can find mathematics:

'As soon as you (the teacher) mentions maths I just get this sick feeling inside and my heart races and I want to cry.'   (Year 5 pupil)

'When Mrs (Smith) asks me anything in maths my head starts spinning. I can see all these columns of numbers spinning round in my brain, but I don't know what to do with them. Then I say the first thing that comes into my head and she shouts at me.'   (Year 3 pupil)

'Sum stress' and school phobia

Before discussing 'sum stress' it is important to understand school phobia and then to establish the specific differences between the two. The term school phobia is rife with controversy among researchers in the mental health community. Bridget Murray (1999) states that the term school phobia dates from 1941 and was first used by Dr Christopher Kearney (University of Nevada) to describe an over-dependent mother–child relationship. It has since become a general term for any problem involving absenteeism.

The pupils that we define as suffering from 'sum stress' differ from those who are school phobic or school 'refusers'. They enjoy school and are usually good attendees. They differ from other pupils only because they have an unusual level of anxiety about mathematics lessons, which results in a lack of success and often low self-esteem. The identification of what is causing a pupil to fail in mathematics is vital if they are to be helped.

Pupils' failure to succeed in mathematics

A number of pupils fail to progress or constantly underachieve in mathematics while reaching a high level in other subjects: 'With such children normal teaching procedures and remedial strategies even of the most enlightened type do not seem enough' (Richards 1982: 77). All teachers will at some point have taught children like this, children who, despite the concentrated efforts of everyone concerned, seem unable to grasp the concepts being taught. Many of these pupils may manage to hide their problems most of the time: 'It is surprising how pupils can conceal their difficulties and get by with alternative strategies – such as counting on their fingers or copying from their neighbours' (Richards 1982: 77). As Richards also points out: 'It is also unfortunate that we sometimes accept the common "I just can't do mathematics" excuse' (1982: 77). This is certainly much more socially acceptable than a similar response about other subjects, and should trigger further examination of the situation. We should never accept that some pupils 'just can't do mathematics'.

Why pupils are failing in mathematics

The reasons why pupils fail to succeed in mathematics are varied. Richards outlines the following bullet points as possible causes of mathematical underachievement. Our comments are in italics:

- Poor teaching
  This is a loaded issue; it will include the few poor teachers often discussed in the media but more importantly refers to poor mathematics teaching. We have discussed examples of poor practice, which can result in low confidence. We discuss later why authoritarian approaches may make it difficult for pupils to progress mathematically.
- Lack of motivation
  The reasons for poor motivation are varied. A well motivated, positive teacher will normally be able to stimulate pupils to do well in mathematics, but other factors are important. The whole-school ethos, attitudes of parents and other adults and other factors all have a role in motivating pupils.
- Inadequate learning of basic concepts
  Pupils may have failed to learn the basic concepts upon which the rest of their mathematical knowledge is constructed. It may be that pupils have missed some schooling for family or medical reasons, that they have changed schools or even countries, that their attitude was poor during their earlier schooling or that they had a clash with a particular teacher early in their school career. Whatever the reason for this 'gap' in the pupils' understanding, taking steps to help pupils to understand the basic concepts is vital, enabling them to develop further mathematically.
- Serious anxiety
  Anxiety can be either the cause of failure or caused by failure, but either is damaging to pupils.

Anxiety and mathematics

Many emotions are triggered at school and these can affect learning in both positive and negative ways. Figure 7.1 shows one pupil's illustration of the emotions she goes through on a daily basis. She suffers from 'sum stress' and was asked to produce a board game showing how school mathematics made her feel.

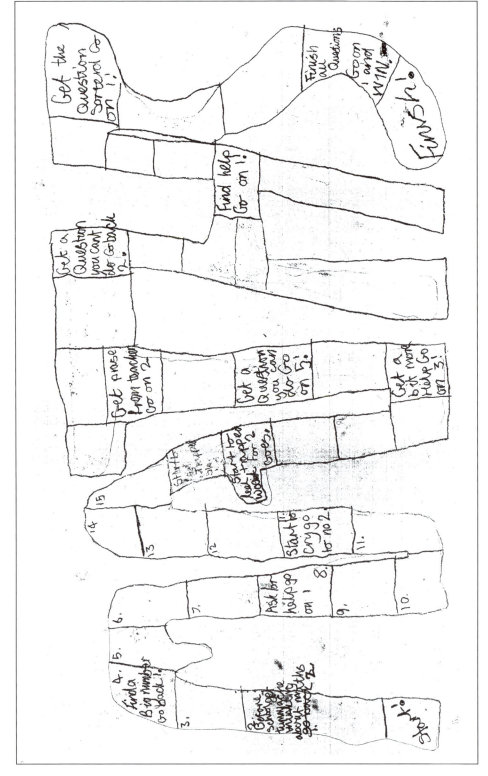

Figure 7.1 Child's illustration of 'sum stress'

Figure 7.2 illustrates how emotions affect the learning process. It is clear that fear leads pupils towards mathematical confusion and possible 'sum stress'. It also shows how pleasure or enjoyment leads pupils towards the goal state of mathematical understanding. These figures highlight the importance of dealing with 'sum stress' and fear as soon as possible, both for the sake of the clearly distressed child in Figure 7.1 and the learning of mathematics in Figure 7.2.

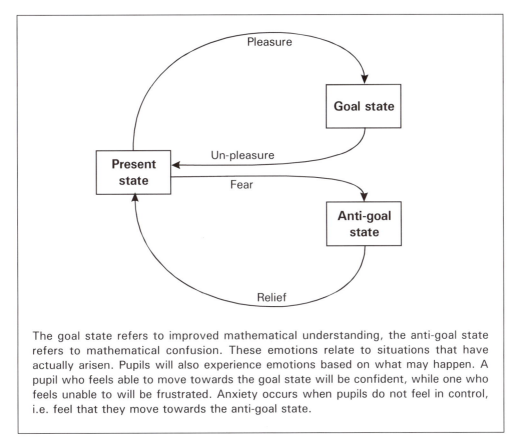

The goal state refers to improved mathematical understanding, the anti-goal state refers to mathematical confusion. These emotions relate to situations that have actually arisen. Pupils will also experience emotions based on what may happen. A pupil who feels able to move towards the goal state will be confident, while one who feels unable to will be frustrated. Anxiety occurs when pupils do not feel in control, i.e. feel that they move towards the anti-goal state.

Figure 7.2 Categories of emotion (Honeyford and Fraser, after Skemp 1989)

Reasons for 'sum stress'

… that anxiety, once present, could bring about a vicious circle of cause and affect in the mathematical-learning situation. On the principle that prevention is better than cure, we should look now for the causes which may introduce anxiety in the first instance.

(Skemp 1986: 121)

The reasons for 'sum stress' are many and varied. They can only really be established through spending time discussing them with individual pupils, and specialist help may be required. Some typical reasons are:

- failure in the past;
- parental pressure;
- low status given to mathematics by parents;
- parent suffers from 'sum stress';
- one very bad experience in a mathematics lesson;
- lack of confidence;
- relationship with current or previous mathematics teacher; and
- physical problem, such as dyspraxia, dyslexia, poor eyesight, etc.

Skemp proposes a reason for 'sum stress' which is more deep rooted, caused by a fundamental flaw in the way some mathematics has been 'traditionally' taught. This also explains why 'sum stress' can suddenly affect pupils, and why the sufferers often seem to be very able children who had previously been mathematically successful. He explains that some able children: 'inevitably reach a stage at which their apparent success inevitably deserts them. Try as they may, they can no longer "get all their sums right"' (Skemp 1986: 123). The reason behind this situation is that much mathematics has traditionally been taught by rote learning. Skemp states that: 'Initially it [rote learning] may well not be accompanied by anxiety, perhaps quite the opposite. Well memorised multiplication tables, resulting in a column of neat red ticks, are rewarding to the teacher and student alike' (Skemp 1986: 122). However, as mathematics becomes more complex it becomes impossible for the pupil to remember all the rules and thus failure begins. Additionally, learnt routines will not enable the pupil to deal with all the mathematical problems they are faced with. This places the pupil in a very awkward situation, particularly when the teacher does not identify the problem. This can lead to anxiety surrounding mathematics.

The introduction of the National Numeracy Strategy should prevent this problem arising, as it prescribes a form of learning based on understanding, not simple recall of facts. For example, children are encouraged to discuss their methods of carrying out a calculation and to use non-standard approaches. 'Sum stress' sufferers we have worked with have found this less stressful, taking away the pressures of setting out standard methods. This will prevent situations like the one below arising.

Pupil: How do I do this one?

Teacher: I shouldn't need to help you with that. You have worked out sums like that before for me.

Pupil: I know Miss. The answer is 83, but I can't remember how to set it out in my book.

(Year 3 pupil)

Teachers' relationship with anxiety

Teachers can compensate for anxiety in mathematics lessons:

> In the course of my education, I had one teacher in particular who strove to provide this emotional support. He tried to create as relaxed an atmosphere as possible, and tried to encourage everyone to make some contribution, no matter how small, without actually putting pressure on anyone to do so.... Thus, emotional support was provided by the teacher and the other pupils.
>
> (Skemp 1989: 199)

However, teachers can also add to or even cause a pupil's anxiety:

> If I did not understand his explanation of a point, instead of explaining it again slowly or in a different way, he seemed to just shout louder and thump his hand on the desk in emphasis of certain points.　(Skemp 1989: 199)

> When you don't know the answer in maths my teacher gets really mad. It's like she thinks you are deliberately getting it wrong. I do OK in other things but in maths I am stupid.　(Year 4 pupil)

In the positive school experience example above a 'relaxed atmosphere' is mentioned. This is easy to say but difficult to achieve: 'The risks inherent in most learning situations can be diminished by good management' (Skemp 1989: 205) Points 1 to 5 below are Skemp's recommendations. Our comments and explanations are in italics.

1. Distinguish between positional authority and authority of knowledge.

   The difference between these two is that positional authority refers to the teacher being 'respected' because they hold a position of authority, and what they say is correct must be right. Authority of knowledge is based on the pupils respecting the fact that the teacher knows more mathematics than they do and learning from this. The difference is subtle but makes a tremendous difference to the pupil–teacher relationship because pupils recognising authority of knowledge are more likely to feel comfortable asking for help and support with their work. In these situations the teacher is more of a facilitator or critical friend than a pedagogue.

2. Provide emotional support for learning.

   This refers to a positive school and classroom ethos where everyone is valued and no one is ridiculed for making mistakes. This is discussed further later in the chapter.

3. Allow time to think.

   Time pressures can reduce anyone's ability to think clearly and to achieve their best. Allowing pupils time to think about the strategies they use and to reflect on them will help reduce their anxieties.

4. Provide opportunities for consolidating newly learnt material before moving on to new topics.

   New concepts and ideas need to be reflected on and practised before they become a part of an individual's mathematical knowledge that is ready to be built on further. This is particularly relevant in light of the National Numeracy Strategy, because pupils are expected to move on after a specific time, irrespective of whether or not they have grasped the concepts being studied. It is important to ensure that appropriate work is set to ensure that the pupils have some experience of success and enjoyment before moving on. This requires careful planning and differentiation.

5. Sometimes allow children to work in areas with which they are comfortably familiar.

   If pupils are given to time to practise areas in which they are confident, particularly if the work is interesting and enjoyable to them (e.g. investigations, ICT based work and mathematical games), their confidence and enjoyment can grow.

Other methods of reducing 'sum stress'

The areas outlined below are all areas that are basically good practice. They are included here because 'sum stress' sufferers are often more sensitive than other pupils to the methods of teaching and the atmosphere in the classroom.

Creating the right environment

This is an awkward area to address and has no simple answers. Personal, social and health education (PSHE) activities such as 'circle time' can help raise pupils' self-esteem and are not out of place in mathematics lessons. Additionally, pupils sitting in a circle are ideally located for many Mental Maths activities. Valuing all the pupils' contributions increases their confidence. Games which allow pupils to spot the teacher's deliberate (or accidental!) mistakes can help demonstrate, in a non-threatening manner, how mistakes are made and also allow modelling of how to avoid or rectify them.

Giving mathematics status

This point may seem odd because mathematics takes up such a large part of the school week and is seen as important by most parents and teachers. However, it is often fitted into an isolated time and is then 'put away until the next lesson'. Having the mathematics equipment on display in a dedicated mathematics area, perhaps similar to a book corner, not only allows the pupils access to it when they need it, but also gives the subject some form of credence. The same is true of mathematics displays, which can be discussed, shared and explored, and of work that can be shown in assembly. Status is also achieved when the pupils understand how mathematics is used in other contexts. Pointing out to pupils that they do mathematics all the time without even realising it helps with this process. Consider measuring in design and technology, studying climate graphs in geography, using repeating patterns in art, doing orienteering in physical education, etc.

Giving different work equal status

The low status of Mental Maths, in comparison to pages of ticks, is a situation that will gradually improve as the National Numeracy Strategy becomes familiar to pupils, but the situation needs to be addressed when the pupils ask 'Can we go and do our work now?' towards the end of a Mental Maths session. The reason that pupils do not always value the Mental Maths session may be either that it was too much fun to be 'work' or a feeling that they need to get some ticks in their books to gain a sense of achievement. Either way the teacher needs to value the work carried out in this part of the lesson to allow the pupils to enjoy and be proud of their success.

Having appropriate equipment available

Pupils need to have access to the appropriate equipment to carry out many mathematical activities. It should be clean, useful and readily to hand to allow it to become an invisible tool for learning. Where possible pupils should have access to a choice of apparatus, such as those outlined in Appendix 5.

Using a gentle approach to start with

'Sum stress' sufferers often find the beginnings of lessons very difficult. The Mental Maths starter, outlined in the National Numeracy Strategy, could prove very problematic if not approached carefully (see Chapter 3). Some children seem to have a great deal of security when presented with hundreds, tens and units sums on paper and can feel lost if these are taken away from them. The feeling of success from receiving a page of ticks for a task that does not really stretch them academically can easily be replaced by anxiety. Simple activities such as choosing their favourite number, then discussing why, then finding simple sums which equate to it before discussing its properties can provide a gentle introduction to Mental Maths. Starting the work with a small group before moving on to whole-class activities may also be successful.

Encouraging discussion

It is very easy to feel that a high noise level in a room means an absence of learning. A balance needs to be found between noise reaching an unacceptable level and allowing discussion. If the class are sitting in silence they are not developing their mathematical vocabulary and thought processes through discussion with their peers, but if the noise level is too high they are unable to concentrate or listen to instructions from the teacher and some children may find this causes anxiety.

Marking

Marking of work is important and there is no avoiding this. The point here is that 'sum stress' sufferers can find this process very difficult, as can many children who are not scoring high marks. Teachers need to consider how to make this process less upsetting. By changing the way in which work is marked the process can be made less threatening and more useful to pupils and parents. It is interesting that 'sum stress' sufferers have anxiety only about mathematics and there may be a link with the unique way in which mathematics is marked. It is usual for mathematics work to be marked either correct or incorrect, with no middle ground. Pupils can respond well to marking incorrect answers with a question mark, rather than with a cross. This allows them to go back and re-examine their answers without feeling that they have failed. Pupils may have completed part of a sum correctly, or used a good method and simply made a calculating error, and this deserves some status even though the answer is incorrect. Other strategies which can help are marking in a more neutral colour than red; perhaps even using pencil in pupils' books so they do not feel that their work is permanently damaged by a wrong answer. It can also be unhelpful to give pupils a mark out of ten, because this simply restates a fact that they are already aware of: 'so constructive written comments are more helpful than mere ticks and crosses, or scores "out of ten"' (DfEE 1999c: 35).

Setting

This is something of a double-edged sword. Pupils who are struggling in mathematics may feel supported by being grouped with other less able children, or may feel humiliated by being in the 'bottom' set or not being in the 'top' group. Mixed ability groupings within a class (which can be varied depending on the mathematical area being studied) or parallel sets can help this situation. The whole-school ethos will also affect this dramatically.

Dyscalculia

Despite all these measures, some children may still fail to achieve success in mathematics. Some will suffer anxiety because of this and others will simply not enjoy it. In such circumstances it is possible that the pupil has a medical barrier to their learning. This could be one of the general conditions such as dyspraxia or poor eyesight, or dyscalculia, which specifically causes problems in mathematics.

Dyscalculia is much less widely publicised and recognised than dyslexia. It is identified by Kosc (1974, cited in Richards 1982) as 'disorders of mathematical ability which are a consequence of heredity or congenital impairment of the growth dynamics of the brain centres' (cited in Richards 1982: 78). Unfortunately, according to Richards, there are so many inconsistencies in definitions and methods of intervention that 'at present there does not appear to be a well enough defined method of diagnosis to provide the classroom teacher with a useful and effective tool in identifying such disorders' (1982: 78) The major difficulty is that the term dyscalculia is often used to describe the result rather than the cause of mathematical failure and this is 'not only unproductive, but potentially harmful' (Richards 1982: 78).

While these issues remain, dyscalculia is too broad an area to be fully addressed in this book. The approaches taken to dyscalculia will vary between local education authorities, schools and individual teachers. The most important thing from our point of view is not to discount dyscalculia from the equation, but to rule out other areas of mathematics failure before jumping to any conclusions.

Conclusion

'Sum stress' is a major problem for some children. Whether their anxieties are caused by mathematical difficulties, or are the cause of them, they need to be addressed. Finding the causes of mathematical failure may be a lengthy process but is vital if solutions are to be found. Parents and teachers have a major role to play in helping pupils to overcome their problems and to find enjoyment in numeracy. This is particularly important as, when 'sum stress' sufferers have their own children, they will not be in a position to help them and indeed may find themselves passing on their fears.

Teachers and parents must be aware of pupils as individuals and strive to provide a supportive environment for them to work in. A final point is that this can be a very sensitive area. Both parents and teachers need to ensure that they take the issue seriously without making the situation worse. For some pupils 'sum stress' may be a manifestation of problems elsewhere.

CHAPTER 8

Developing home–school links

Mathematics education can be problematic for many parents and unfortunately the new approach to mathematics outlined in the National Numeracy Strategy may not improve this initially, although it is clearly seen as important by the Department for Education and Employment (DfEE). In this chapter we address the issues for schools attempting to improve their links with parents. We examine how these links are made and examine their importance.

Why involve the family?

The empowerment of parents helps children develop their mathematics and view it without anxiety. This enables parents and children to see mathematics as an enjoyable experience, which relates to everyday life. Effective partnership between parents and school is crucial to increasing enjoyment of mathematics for all parties involved.

The National Numeracy Strategy identifies the key reasons for involving the family:

- the involvement of parents is crucial to children's educational achievement;
- most parents want to help their child but many don't know how;
- teachers can affect how much and how effectively parents work with their child;
- sending work home will not, on its own, raise children's achievement;
- teachers can establish the nature and quality of what is sent home, allowing for feedback and discussion.   (DfEE 1999a: 51)

The reasons outlined in the strategy are all concerned with raising 'standards' in numeracy. In addition to standards, we are also concerned with raising the status and enjoyment of mathematics by all parties concerned.

New approach – new problems

Approaches to teaching outlined in the National Numeracy Strategy are different to the ways of learning mathematics experienced by most parents and teachers. Such differences are not problems in themselves but can be the cause them, if misunderstood. The danger is that the new methods of teaching may be perceived as a drop in standards, although this will certainly not be the case.

- The flexible approach to written methods and the emphasis on pupils exploring numbers will not result in neat pages of identically presented sums, each one ticked neatly in red ink with a gold star and '10/10' written beautifully at the bottom of the page.

  If parents expect to receive a pupil's book home once a week with pages of beautifully laid out sums, then a page of work that is presented in a seemingly haphazard way may cause concern. If parents try to rectify this 'problem' by showing pupils how they carry out a particular operation, or how their work 'should be' set out, confusion can arise.

- The increased time spent discussing work orally will mean that less work is formally written out, so the children will not fill as many exercise books as before.

  If the pupil has produced less written work than parents expect (based on their own experience or perhaps the work carried out by older siblings) they may start to feel that things are *going wrong* for their children, or that their children are having problems at school. Anticipating and dealing with this problem in advance can prevent a lot of distress for all concerned.

- Using flexible approaches that work with the child's intuitive method means that the child can make excellent progress without ever feeling that they are under pressure.

  This may not sound like a problem but it may be. Children whose experience of mathematics at school is positive may really enjoy their lessons. This is excellent news for the child and their learning, but may lead parents to feeling that their child is not being 'pushed'. Consider a quote from a parent at a whole-school meeting on the National Numeracy Strategy on learning that long division was going to be taught in a new way to Year 5: 'Well that is just stupid, they keep making things easier. I had to do it the hard way, why shouldn't they?' This illustrates the problems teachers may come up against.

  Mathematics should not be needlessly hard. This sounds trivial but many parents, and indeed some teachers, do not yet appreciate the reasons behind the alternative methods outlined in the National Numeracy Strategy. They view them as 'another new initiative' or simply 'change for the sake of change' rather than a means of allowing more children to do harder mathematics. These problems arise from people who may have struggled with mathematics themselves. Another set of problems comes from those who found mathematics easy at school; those for whom School Mathematics Project (SMP) cards were a positive experience. It is easy to forget that for many people school mathematics was not a good experience, which is why change became necessary. The view that 'traditional' is best is both commonplace and potentially dangerous and so must be addressed.

- Investigations will not necessarily have a mathematical content that is clear to the casual observer.

   Mathematics investigations (see Chapter 6) have huge benefits in school mathematics. They enable pupils to use and apply their mathematical knowledge and are very popular with the majority of pupils. However, many parents do not see these as being proper mathematics and have no understanding of why schools use them. This lack of understanding can lead to links not being made and lack of support from home.

New approach – old problems

- Parents may not feel confident helping their children.

   Many parents want to help their children with their school mathematics but do not know how. This may be because their own experience of mathematics is limited or they feel it is a long time since they did any mathematics. Aspects of mathematics were approached differently when they were at school and other parts were not covered at all. This area is already an issue for many parents who are unsure of how to approach subtraction with exchange because they learnt a different method when they were at school (see Figure 8.1). The same is true of work on 'shape and space', because many parents will never have studied this at school, or will have done so at a later stage as geometry and trigonometry. Confidence plays a major role in parents' effectiveness when working with their

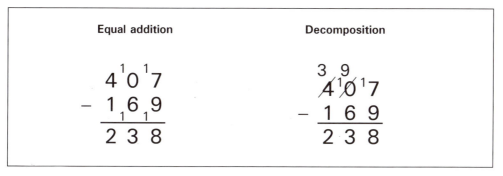

Figure 8.1 Two methods of subtraction. Which way were you taught?

children and parents not understanding the new written methods could further reduce this.

- Parents' own mathematics

    The acceptability in society of being 'bad at maths' is a problem (see page 3). Parents often say, 'Well, I was never any good at maths when I was at school', in a way that you could never imagine people saying about reading. This statement is often coupled with defensiveness and the sentence ends with 'and I've done all right!' Parents may have suffered 'sum stress' as children, and may never have overcome their difficulties. Their fears can be unconsciously passed on to their children or they may be unable to help their children because of their own lack of confidence.

There is often an undercurrent which suggests that mathematics is either not important, or is something that you can't really learn – you are born being good at it. The National Numeracy Strategy is an attempt to ensure that everybody has the opportunity both to be good at and to enjoy mathematics.

A positive approach for schools

Parents are a valuable resource in the education of pupils. They need to be informed, valued and harnessed by schools to support pupils in their enjoyment of and success in mathematics. The ideas below are ways of addressing the issues outlined previously. Each problem is not matched to a specific solution, as the issues involved are much more complex than that. As Bill Rogers, the famous Australian educator, said, 'For every complex problem there is a simple solution and it is WRONG!' (Rogers 1999). Outlined here is a range of strategies that will help to address the problems when used appropriately.

Parents meetings

A meeting, or series of meetings and workshops, for all the interested parents may well be a very good starting point for explaining some of the ways in which your school tackles the teaching of mathematics. Some of the points that could be addressed are:

- the structure of mathematics lessons;
- what Mental Maths is;
- the new written methods;
- why there is a new approach to teaching mathematics; and
- the reasons for investigations.

Organising and planning meetings can be very time consuming but the time spent explaining these areas to parents may help prevent problems later. During these meetings try to generate discussion among parents as to how they carry out different calculations. This will allow them to see that not everyone calculates in exactly the same way. A discussion or brainstorm of their memories of school mathematics may be fruitful (or painful!).

Attracting parents to evening meetings can be difficult and novel solutions sometimes need to be tried. For example, one school, which was struggling to attract parents to its evening meetings, laid on meals for all those attending, provided from the school canteen. Other schools have used the offer of a free glass of wine, or free entry into a raffle, as a way of trying to attract parents. However, schools should not despair. Mathematics meetings often attract a good audience because of the importance placed on mathematics by parents. Using this enthusiasm to take the parent body wholeheartedly into the National Numeracy Strategy is crucial.

Booklets

Not all parents will be able to attend a meeting and even those who do will benefit from having a document to refer back to. Many parents are used to receiving reams of paper from their children's school on a termly basis and others find that letters sent home with children do not reach their intended audience! For this reason care should be taken when producing a guide for parents to ensure that when completed it has enough status for the pupils and parents to take care of it and read it. This is perhaps best achieved by having some form of semi-rigid binding or cover on the completed document. Areas that could be usefully included in such a booklet include those outlined in Figure 8.2.

Other school events

Despite all your efforts, there will be some parents who do not or cannot attend the meetings or read the booklets. These parents may, however, attend other school events such as parents evenings, assemblies, plays, fêtes and jumble sales. A large mathematics display showing resources and the strategies outlined in the National Numeracy Strategy can reach the parents the other methods did not, as well as raising the status of mathematics among other parents and pupils.

Figure 8.2 Maths booklet: cover and contents page

Parents as a resource

Parents are a valuable resource and schools can often make more use of them. They can be used in many ways, including:

- for technical help with ICT;
- to work with a small group;
- to share experiences of when they use mathematics in the real world;
- to support individual pupils; and
- to help make resources.

The benefits of bringing parents into school should be felt by schools, parents and teachers alike. Parents who have helped to make resources are likely to be more interested in how they will be used in class and therefore are more likely to understand their use. They may also feel more able to make their own suggestions or to try out ideas to help their own children. Parents who become proficient working with an individual child or small group are a great asset in the classroom, taking some pressure off the teacher and providing more rapid feedback for the pupils. They may also feel empowered by learning alongside their children and the resulting boost in confidence could help them in other areas. As one parent, working as a learning support assistant said to me, 'This job is wonderful. I feel as if I am learning as much as they (the children) are, but then I feel I am able to help them better'. This is a good example of schools and parents working together and supporting lifelong learning.

Family numeracy projects

Family numeracy projects can be organised in many ways. Their aim is to improve the numeracy of parents and to use this to help improve the children's performance. They can also harness the skills of already numerate parents to help pupils and other parents improve their skills in this area. Government funding may be available to help schools establish these projects. Case Study 4 outlines how one school ran its project.

Maths days and trails

Maths days and trails are a useful way of raising the status of mathematics in a fun way that involves the wider community, including parents. Maths trails consist of mathematical activities laid out throughout the school buildings, grounds or both. Maths days are simply whole days devoted to mathematics related activities. They can take the form of extended investigations or projects, challenges between classes, mathematical themes in other lessons, etc. Inviting guest speakers to such days can bring an added interest to mathematics in a school. They are becoming more difficult to organise as the curriculum becomes more and more pressurised, but have many positive benefits. They are useful because they can help encourage parents into school without the pressure of a regular time commitment and otherwise reluctant parents become involved in a mathematics activity without requiring a great deal of mathematical knowledge.

Conclusion

Parents should work in partnership with teachers to support children's learning of mathematics. Building and maintaining this link is time consuming and may at times seem like a thankless task, but effective partnerships between home and schools are

Case Study 4

The project was externally funded and ran for ten weeks. The school is a primary school in a multicultural area. The parents attracted by the project were mixed in terms of mathematical ability, ranging from one with a degree in mathematics from Oxford to those who found basic calculations challenging. The cultural diversity of the area was unfortunately not reflected in those who attended. The structure was as follows:

Tuesday
Parents worked with a teacher (released from their class for half a day) in the afternoon. The teacher and parents worked together on a mathematical area or concept (e.g. shape or multiplication) at their level. This helped them to develop confidence in mathematics and to work together. Next the parents worked with the support of the teacher to produce resources that they could use with their own children to teach them about the mathematics they had been doing. These resources (see Appendix 6) were simple but effective and reflected the parents' knowledge of their children's interests in a way that a mathematics scheme could not. They are also suitable for inclusion in a mathematics booklet as outlined in Figure 8.2.

Thursday
The parents met with their children and the teacher (again released for half a day). The parents then used the resources they had created and the knowledge gained during Tuesday's session to teach their children at an appropriate level.

Results
The parents and teacher involved in the project reported that they found the experience valuable. The parents' confidence in helping their children was greatly improved. The class teachers of the pupils involved in the project reported that they had found the pupils to be more confident and enthusiastic about mathematics than their peers who were not involved.

The teacher who ran the project stated that the process was very time consuming and that the pressures involved might be reduced if the workload was shared by more than one teacher, or if more release time was available.

incredibly valuable and really help children to achieve their potential. Obviously not all the ideas outlined in this chapter need to be included in any one school, but the underlying philosophy has a place in every school.

Questions and simple activities for use in teaching Mental Maths

- What sums make 10, 20, 100?, and so on.

- Large-scale number work:
  - 100 square carpet tiles with pupils moving on tiles to undertake calculation
  - human number line
  - washing line with numbers pegged to it which can be moved and sorted.

- Three coins in my pocket:
  - What are they?
  - How much could I have?
  - What is the least amount I could have?

- How did you do that sum? Could you have done it another way?

- Here are four digits:
  - What sums and answers can you make with any operation?
  - What sums and answers can you make only using multiplication, etc.?
  - What is the largest/smallest answer?

- Using the numbers in today's date, what numbers can you make?

- What number am I thinking of (using questions that can only be answered yes or no)?

- Function machines (see Chapter 5).

- Guess my rule (e.g. divides exactly by 6). Pupils suggest numbers and are told 'Yes' if they fit the teacher's rule.

- How many children in the class:
  - are having school dinners?
  - bring sandwiches, etc.?

- Estimating games:
- How many sweets are there in a jar?
- How many crisps in a packet?
- How many Smarties in a tube?

- Reading and chanting of tables, forwards/backwards, round a circle, using a counting stick etc.

- Using a Gattengo chart (see Appendix 7), reading of hundreds, thousands, tenths, etc.

- Chanting numbers in steps of 2, 3, 4, …10, etc.:
- forwards/backwards
- starting at different numbers (e.g. in 3s from 15).

- Continuing patterns.

- Rounding up and down:
- give me 48 to the nearest 10
- 280 to the nearest 100, etc.

- Spot the missing number in a sum/sequence.

- Number bond chants. Teacher says a number, the pupils call back the number it must be added to to make 10 or 100.

- How many minutes to the next hour if the minute hand is on…?

- Tables Bingo: the caller uses '2 × 11', '7 – 4', '2 + 3', etc.

- Place Value Bingo: 4 units and 5 tens.

- Conversions:
- How many centimetres in 4 metres?
- How many pounds in 134 pence?

- Singing number rhymes.

- Dominoes: various types from fractions and decimals to tables.

Activities using arrow cards, digit cards or number fans

- Use cards to show numbers represented by Dienes material.
- Use cards to answer:

$40 + 3$ $700 + 8$

$300 + 20 + 6$ 6×5, etc.

- In the nine times table show me:
- an even number
- a prime number.

- What is double/half this number (shown by the teacher)?

- Show me a number with:
- no units
- 6 tens
- no hundreds, etc.

- Make a number between 90 and 100.

- Show me a number which is:
- 1 more than (teacher to say or show number)
- 1 less
- 10 more
- 300 less, etc.

- Make a number which is 6 times bigger than . . . .

- Working with a partner, make two numbers so that they have a difference of 10, 20, etc. Make two numbers which total 100 or 1000.

- Give an approximate answer to 41×39.

- Multiply this number by 25 (perhaps by multiplying first by 100 and then dividing by 4).

Hardware resources and suppliers

Classroom robots

Pip and Pixie
Swallow Systems
134 Cock Lane
High Wycombe
Buckinghamshire HP13 7EA
Tel: 01494 813471
http://www.swallow.co.uk

Roamer
Valiant Technology
3 Grange Mills
Weir Road
London SW12 0NE
Tel: 020 8673 2222
info@valiant-technology.com

Video projectors/OHP overlays

MISCO
Faraday Close
Park Farm Industrial Estate
Wellingborough
Northants. NN8 6XH
Tel: 01933 400400
salesdesk@misco.co.uk
www.misco.co.uk

Simply Computers Ltd
2/3 Forest Works
Forest Road
Walthamstow
London E17 6JF
Tel: 0870 7287000
www.simply.co.uk

Just Projectors
2 Kings Drive Park
Kings Ride
Ascot SL5 8BP
Tel: 07000 587877
sales@projectors.co.uk

PC–TV adaptors

CPC PLC
Faraday Drive
Fulwood
Preston, Lancs.
Tel: 01772 654455
http://www.cpc.co.uk
sales@cpc.co.uk

OHP calculators

Oxford Educational Supplies
Unit 19
Weston Business Park
Weston on the Green
Bicester
Oxon. OX6 8SY
Tel: 01869 344500
sales@Oxford-Educational.co.uk

Interactive whiteboards

Mustard Solutions
2 Sandridge Park
Porters Wood
Valley Road Industrial Estate
St Albans
Hertfordshire AL3 6PH
Tel: 01727 732110
www.mustard-uk.com

Software titles and distributors

Spreadsheets/databases

Datagraph
Topologika
1 South Harbour
Harbour Village
Penryn
Cornwall TR10 8LR
Tel: 01326 377771
sales@topologika.demon.co.uk

Picture Point and Pinpoint
Logotron
124 Cambridge Science Park
Milton Road
Cambridge CB4 0ZS
Tel: 01223 425558
sales@logo.com
www.logo.com

Data Explorer
TAG Developments Ltd
Dept PR102
Freepost SEA1652
25 Pelham Road
Gravesend
Kent DA11 0BR
Tel: 01474 537887
sales@TAGDEV.co.uk
http://www.TAGDEV.co.uk

Number Box, First Workshop and Information Workshop
Black Cat Software
Lion House
Bethel Square
Brecon
Powys LD3 7JP
Tel: 01874 622114
sales@blackcatsoftware.com

Question generators

Hooray for Henrietta
Lander
REM
Freepost
TU823
Great Western House
Langport
Somerset TA10 9BR
Tel: 01458 253636
www.r-e-m.co.uk
sales@r-e-m.co.uk

Megamaths Tables
Logotron

Magic Maths
Published by CCS
Supplied by AVP
School Hill Centre
Chepstow
Monmouthshire NP6 5PH
Tel: 01291 625439
avp@compuserve.com
www.avp.co.uk

Pattern generators

Shropshire Maths Suite
Publication and Design Unit
The Advisory Service
Shirehall
Abbey Foregate
Shrewsbury SY2 6ND
Tel: 01743 254321

Movement/control

Various LOGO packages
Supplied by Logotron
Also available from NRICH website

Numeracy specific

Developing Number
The Association of Teachers of
  Mathematics (ATM)
7 Shaftesbury Street
Derby DE23 8YB
Tel: 01332 346599
atm_maths@compuserve.com

Puzzles

MicroSmile Mathematics Software
Smile Mathematics
Isaac Newton Centre
108A Lancaster Road
London W11 1QS
Tel: 020 7221 8966
smile@rmplc.co.uk
http://www.rmplc.co.uk

Maths Circus
4mation
14 Castle Park Road
Barnstaple
Devon EX32 8PA
Tel: 01271 322974
sales@4mation.co.uk
http://www.4mation.co.uk

Maths Mission: Problem Solving
Granada Learning Ltd – SEMERC
Granada Television
Quay Street
Manchester M60 9EA
Tel: 0161 8272927

Investigations

Breakaway Maths
Granada Learning Ltd

Maths Factory
Sherston
Angel House
Sherston
Malmesbury
Wiltshire SN16 0LH
Tel: 01666 843200
sales@sherston.co.uk
http://www.sherston.co.uk

Giant Killer
Topologika

SEN Support

Times Tabler
Published by Marco Publishing
Supplied by REM

Various Titles
Inclusive Technology
Saddlewoth Business Centre
Delph
Oldham OL3 5DF
Tel: 01487 81790
inclusive@inclusive.co.uk

Simulations

Maths Explorer
Published by YITM
Supplied by AVP

Super Solvers Outnumbered
Published by TLC
Supplied by AVP

Cars; Maths in Motion
Cambridge Software House
P.O. Box 163
Huntingdon
Cambridgeshire PE17 3UR
Tel: 01487 741223
cshsoft@compuserve.com
http://ourworld.compuserve.com/
  homepages/cshsoft

Teachers' notes to accompany investigations

These notes are designed to help teachers when using some of the investigations in Chapter 6 for the first time. Not all solutions are given but the information here should help parents and teachers help children to approach and enjoy the investigations from a position of strength.

Unifix towers investigation

If, as illustrated in Figure 6.1, the first tower, made from only one cube is taken to be $n = 1$, then the number of cubes for the nth position is $3n - 2$.

If the first tower is taken to be $n = 0$, the equation is $3n + 1$.

Crossing rivers investigations

The solution to only one of the investigations is given here as we don't wish to give too much away!

The farmer takes the chicken across leaving the fox with the grain. The farmer comes back. The farmer takes the grain across and brings the chicken back. The farmer leaves the chicken and takes the fox back. The farmer leaves the fox with the grain and returns to collect the chicken.

Milk crate investigation

The first thing to notice about this puzzle is that each row and column must have an even number of bottles in it. Since each row and column is even and must contain an even number of bottles, it follows that they must also contain an even number of gaps. With 18 bottles to consider the puzzle is complex, if you only consider the 6 spaces the puzzle is much simpler. There are many solutions, but only one is given here. Clearly the position of the 'gaps' can be moved to give other solutions.

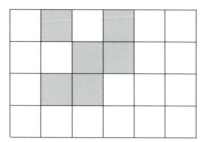

'How many?' investigations

The solutions here will clearly depend on the objects chosen and the area to fill. The complexity increases as the size of the object gets smaller relative to the size of the room. The numbers involved in 'How many shoe boxes will fill this cupboard?' will clearly be smaller than those in 'How many Smarties will fill this room?'.

For most pupils the investigation involves working out what size cuboid an object fills and what size cuboid they are trying to fill. Younger pupils will need to use larger objects to assist with the measuring.

Packaging investigations

These are straightforward.

Real-life context investigations

Teachers may find it helpful to set out simplified lists showing an example of which calculations need to be carried out. A spreadsheet template (See Chapter 5) could also be created.

Mathematical frogs investigation

When pupils (or teachers) investigate this problem for the first time they may feel that it is not possible to complete without the frogs being able to slide forwards and backwards. The simplified version with four frogs and five lily pads may help to show that the problem is in fact possible.

The solution for the four frog investigation is :

G	G	–	R	R
G	–	G	R	R
G	R	G	–	R
G	R	G	R	–
G	R	–	R	G
–	R	G	R	G
R	–	G	R	G
R	R	G	–	G
R	R	–	G	G

A useful starting point is to record the sequence of moves in terms of slides and hops: i.e. S, H, S, H, H, S, H, S.

The solution for five frogs is:

R	R	R	–	G	G	G
R	R	–	R	G	G	G
R	R	G	R	–	G	G
R	R	G	R	G	–	G
R	R	G	–	G	R	G
R	–	G	R	G	R	G
–	R	G	R	G	R	G
G	R	–	R	G	R	G
G	R	G	R	–	R	G
G	R	G	R	G	–	R
G	R	G	–	G	R	R
G	–	G	R	G	R	R
G	G	–	R	G	R	R
G	G	G	R	–	R	R
G	G	G	–	R	R	R

Nimb

This game is appealing at many levels and understanding the ways to always win is not important to all pupils. We do not wish to give too much away, but teachers and pupils could look at the effect of leaving sequences of counters, e.g. 2, 3, 4 or 1, 2, 3, and also leaving equal numbers of counters in two rows.

The mathematics classroom

Equipment list

- 100 squares
- Arrow cards
- Buttons
- Calculators
- Card
- Counters
- Dienes apparatus
- Dice (assorted)
- Dominoes
- Erasers
- Gattengo charts (see Appendix 7)
- Glue
- Graph paper
- Isometric paper
- Mathematics games
- Mirrors
- Money
- Number balances
- Number fans or digit cards
- Number lines, including blank
- Pairs of compasses
- Pencils and pencil sharpeners
- Playing cards
- Rulers, protractors, etc.
- Scales
- Scissors
- Sorting items with Carrol and Venn diagrams
- Squared paper
- String
- Tables charts
- Tangram sets
- Tracing paper
- Unifix squares

Maths equipment suppliers

LDA
Duke Street
Wisbech
Cambs. PE13 2AE
Tel: 01945 463441
ldaorders@compuserve.com

BEAM
Maze Workshops
72a Southgate Road
London N1 3JT
Tel: 020 7684 3330
info@beam.co.uk

Economatics
Epic House
Darnall Road
Attercliffe
Sheffield S9 5AA
Tel: 0114 281 3311
education@economatics.co.uk

Smart Kids (UK) Ltd
169b Main Street
New Greenham Park
Thatcham
Berkshire RG19 6HN

Hope Education
Orb Mill
Huddersfield Road
Oldham
Lancashire OL4 2ST
Tel: 0161 633 6611
enquiries@hope-education.co.uk
www.hope-education.co.uk

Teacher Boards Ltd
Airedale Business Centre
Skipton
North Yorkshire BD23 2TZ
Tel: 01756 700501
sales@teacherboards.co.uk
www.teacherboards.co.uk

PCET
27 Kirchen Road
London W13 0UD
Tel: 020 8567 9206

Philip and Tracey Ltd
North Way
Andover
Hants. SP10 5BA
Tel: 01264 332171
sales@philipandtracey.co.uk
www.philipandtracey.co.uk

Walker Books
87 Vauxhall Walk
London SE11 5HJ
Tel: 020 7792 0909

Sample content for home–school mathematics activities booklet, produced by parents

NUMBER BOOK

My name is _____

I was born on _____

I have _____

Their names are _____

and _____

and _____

and _____

0 1 2 3 4 5 6 7 8 9

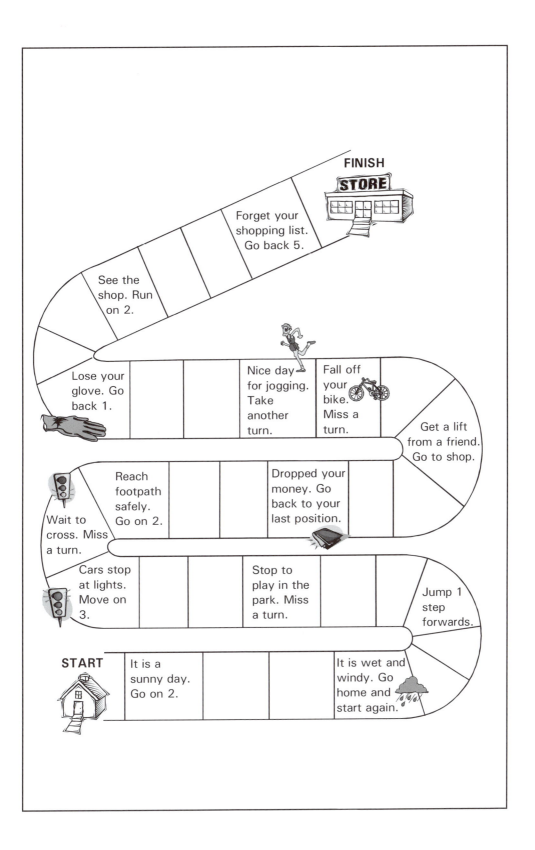

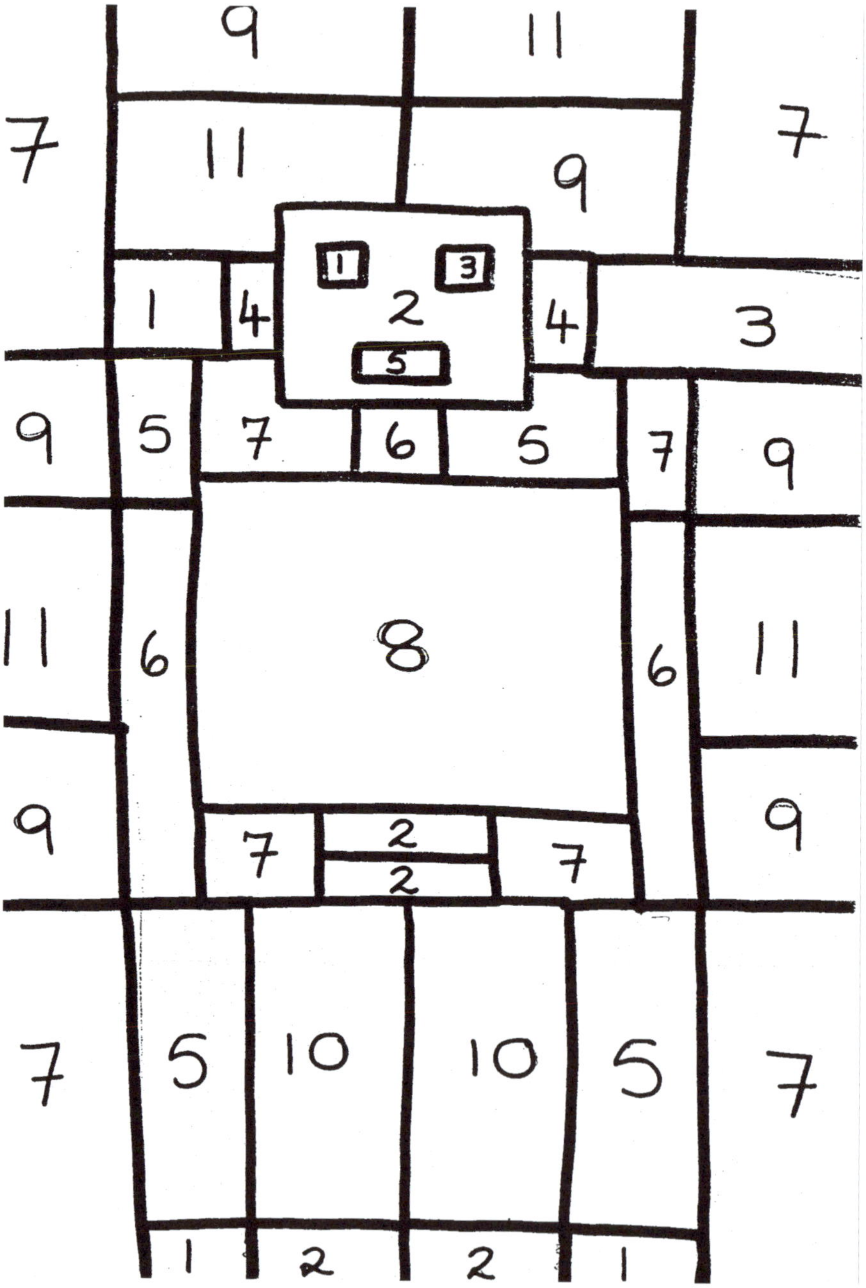
9
11
7
11
9
7
1
1
4
2
3
4
3
5
9
5
7
6
5
7
9
11
6
8
6
11
9
7
2
2
7
9
7
5
10
10
5
7
1
2
2
1

SPECIAL NUMBERS

My house is number _____

My telephone number is _____

Our car number is _____

_____

_____

_____

_____

MY DAY

MY WEEK

Sunday

Monday

Tuesday

Wednesday

Thursday

Friday

Saturday

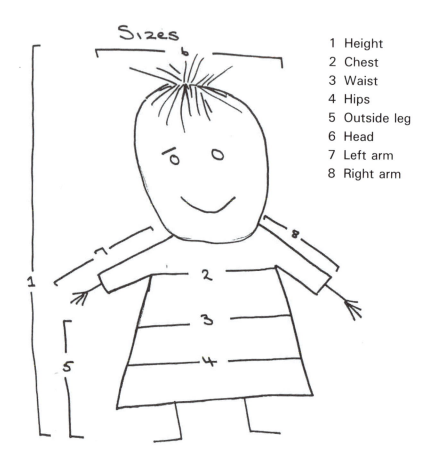

Sizes

1 Height
2 Chest
3 Waist
4 Hips
5 Outside leg
6 Head
7 Left arm
8 Right arm

Measure your friends:

Add: 7 + 8 + 5 + 5

Take away: 3 − 2

Add: 6 + 7 + 4

Take away: 8 − 5

MY SIZE

Today is _____

My height is _____ centimetres.

My foot is _____ centimetres long.

My hand is _____ centimetres long.

My chest is _____ centimetres.

My waist is _____ centimetres.

Colour the picture using this key:

Brown   numbers between 23 and 203
Red   numbers greater than 891
Yellow numbers between 302 and 203

Black   numbers less than 23
Green   numbers less than 891 and bigger than 302

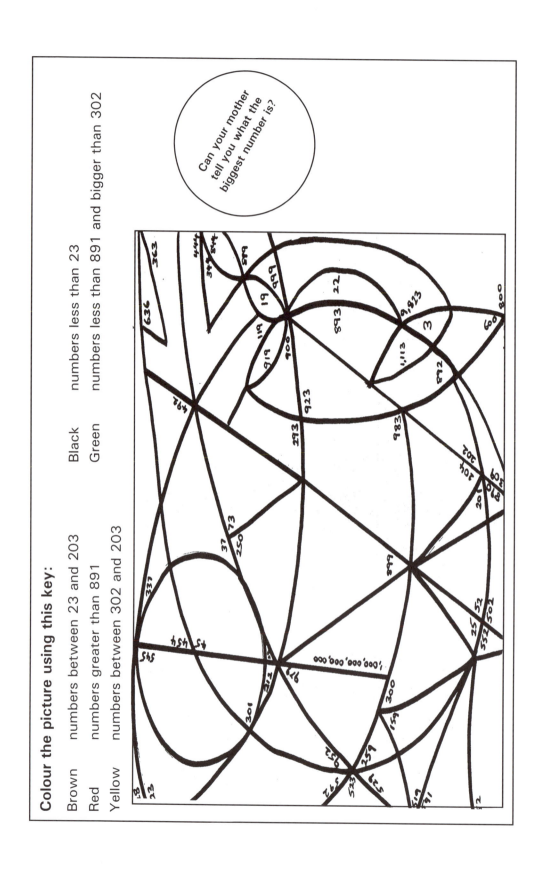

Can your mother tell you what the biggest number is?

Photocopiable classroom resources

Arrow cards

1	0	0	⟋	1	0	⟋	1	⟋
2	0	0	⟋	2	0	⟋	2	⟋
3	0	0	⟋	3	0	⟋	3	⟋
4	0	0	⟋	4	0	⟋	4	⟋
5	0	0	⟋	5	0	⟋	5	⟋
6	0	0	⟋	6	0	⟋	6	⟋
7	0	0	⟋	7	0	⟋	7	⟋
8	0	0	⟋	8	0	⟋	8	⟋
9	0	0	⟋	9	0	⟋	9	⟋

Number fans

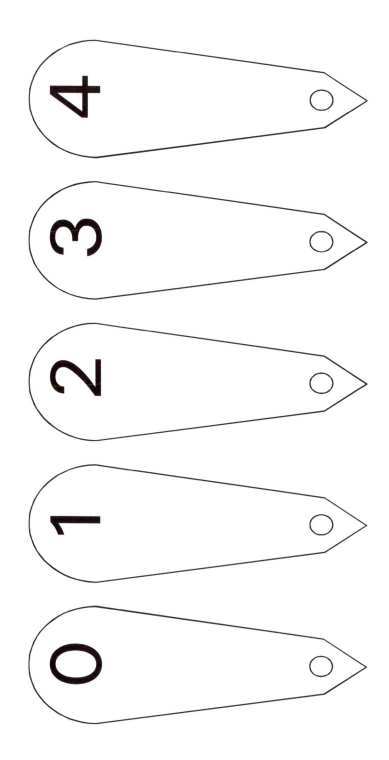

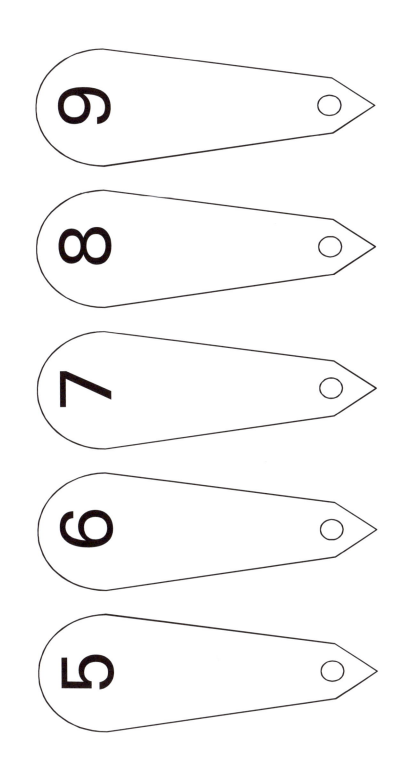

100 square

1	2	3	4	5	6	7	8	9	10
11	12	13	14	15	16	17	18	19	20
21	22	23	24	25	26	27	28	29	30
31	32	33	34	35	36	37	38	39	40
41	42	43	44	45	46	47	48	49	50
51	52	53	54	55	56	57	58	59	60
61	62	63	64	65	66	67	68	69	70
71	72	73	74	75	76	77	78	79	80
81	82	83	84	85	86	87	88	89	90
91	92	93	94	95	96	97	98	99	100

Two examples of Gattengo charts

1	2	3	4	5	6	7	8	9
10	20	30	40	50	60	70	80	90
100	200	300	400	500	600	700	800	900
1000	2000	3000	4000	5000	6000	7000	8000	9000
10000	20000	30000	40000	50000	60000	70000	80000	90000

1	2	3	4	5	6	7	8	9
0.1	0.2	0.3	0.4	0.5	0.6	0.7	0.8	0.9
0.01	0.02	0.03	0.04	0.05	0.06	0.07	0.08	0.09
0.001	0.002	0.003	0.004	0.005	0.006	0.007	0.008	0.009
0.0001	0.0002	0.0003	0.0004	0.0005	0.0006	0.0007	0.0008	0.0009

Epilogue

Our aim when we set out to write this book, as should be clear from the title, was to help parents, teachers and children enjoy numeracy. Many people find that mathematics causes them anxiety and this is clearly not conducive to learning. When all parties involved in mathematics education are confident, relaxed and enjoying the process, learning takes place and achievement follows. We have not set out to give a recipe for success that will work in all situations, but rather to encourage all those involved in the teaching of mathematics to reflect on how they tackle this process and to open themselves to change.

The National Numeracy Strategy is a powerful tool for teachers. It follows closely after the National Literacy Strategy, which has not been popular with all. We believe that the background research, which resulted in its publication, and the lengthy trials that took place prior to its introduction, have helped to create a useful and workable document. The strategy should not therefore be condemned without giving it a chance by those who were unhappy about the National Literacy Strategy.

Encouraging pupils to think about numbers and equipping them with strategies for carrying out mental calculations will help them both in school mathematics and in other areas of their lives. Teaching them to use written methods based on understanding, not rote learning, will also help to reduce errors and increase understanding and enjoyment. It is, after all, very difficult to enjoy something that you have little or no understanding of (except, perhaps, opera!).

We have discussed in some detail how ICT can be used to aid the teaching of mathematics. Clearly, computers cannot replace the teacher in the teaching of mathematics, and nor should they. They can, however, provide innovative ways of displaying information to capture the imagination of pupils and to stimulate the enjoyment we feel so passionately about. They can also provide pupils with the tools necessary to test their own ideas and act as impartial judges for pupils playing mathematical games.

It is our belief that parents should be encouraged to become active partners in the education of their children. This is not something that will happen overnight and schools will need to work hard to build these home–school links. This means much more than simply 'getting parents to sign' home–school agreements. They must be informed and encouraged to work with their children on mathematics activities, both at home and in school. Once again, this process is lengthy but the results are worth-while.

'Sum stress' is still a problem for many pupils and, indeed, parents and teachers. Although the National Numeracy Strategy will help reduce the pressure on children to learn particular methods by rote, it will not eliminate 'sum stress' by itself. Teach-ers need to understand that anxiety is a problem for some pupils and establish what can be done to help these pupils. If mathematics lessons can be made enjoyable through the use of games and interesting resources, pupils will relax and learn more, even if this is not the impression given to visitors to the school who hear laughter coming from the room.

If, by reading this book, teachers and parents reflect on the mathematics they were taught and that they teach, and through discussion begin to develop an understanding that mathematics can and should be an enjoyable activity, we will be very satisfied. We welcome any comments and suggestions through our website (http://members.aol.com/garethhon/) and look forward to hearing from you.

Hamish Fraser and Gareth Honeyford
February 2000

Bibliography

Askew, M. *et al.* (1996) *Number at Key Stage 2*. London: BEAM.

Askew, M. *et al.* (1997) Effective Teachers of Numeracy, Final Report (Feb 1997). London: King's College, London.

Association of Teachers of Mathematics (1999) *Developing Number Instruction Booklet*. Derby: ATM.

Briggs, M. and Crook, J. (1991) 'Bags and baggage', in Love, E. and Pimm, D. (eds) *Teaching and Learning Mathematics*. London: Hodder and Stoughton.

Buxton, L. (1981) *Do you Panic about Maths?* London: Heinemann.

Carvel, J. (1999) 'Teachers too ashamed to admit inability in maths', *Guardian*, 2 September.

Cockcroft, W. H. (1982) *Mathematics Counts. Report of the Committee of Inquiry into the Teaching of Mathematics under the Chairmanship of Dr. W. H. Cockcroft*. London: HMSO.

Corfield, A. (1999) *Why Teach Mental Mathematics?* Derby: ATM.

DfEE (1998) Circular 4/98. London: HMSO.

DfEE (1999a) Course Booklet. London: DfEE Publications.

DfEE (1999b) *Reasoning about Numbers, with Challenges and Simplifications*. London: DfEE Publications.

DfEE (1999c) *National Numeracy Strategy*. London: DfEE Publications.

Fraser, H. (1998) 'Pressure for success 5, success 0', *Questions of Primary Maths and Science*, January 1998, 22–3.

Fraser, H. (2000) 'Mathematics and ICT', in Leask, M. and Meadows, R. (eds) *Teaching and Learning with ICT in the Primary School*, 81–96. London: Routledge.

Hannaford, C. (1999) 'Class talk', *New Scientist* **163**(2201), 28 August, 46–7.

Hargreaves, A. (1994) *Changing Teachers Changing Times*. London: Cassell.

Haylock, D. (1995) *Mathematics Explained for Primary Teachers*. London: Paul Chapman Publishing.

Haylock, D. and Cockburn, A. (1989) *Understanding Early Years Mathematics*. London: Paul Chapman Publishing.

Murray, B. (1999) American Psychological Society Website, http://www.apa.org/monitor/sep97/define.html (accessed August 1999)

OFSTED (1997) *The Teaching of Number in Three Inner-urban LEAs*, reference: 115/97/DS. London: OFSTED.

Richards, P. (1982) 'Difficulties in learning mathematics', in Cornelius, M. (ed.) *Teaching Mathematics*, 59–80. London & Canberra: Croom Helm.

Rogers, B. (1999) Cracking the Hard Class, seminar, 14 June, School of Education, University of Cambridge.

SCRE (1995) 'Primary teachers need help to teach science', press release 95/001, 6 November 1995.

Sewell, B. (1981) *Use of Mathematics by Adults in Daily Life*. Leicester, Advisory Council for Adult and Continuing Education.

Skemp, R. R. (1986) *The Psychology of Learning Mathematics*. Harmondsworth: Penguin.

Skemp, R. R. (1989) *Mathematics in the Primary School*. London: Routledge.

Welch, W. M. (1889) 'How to organise, classify and teach a country school', in Bidwell, J. K. and Clason, R. G. (1970) *Readings in the History of Mathematics Education*. Washington DC: The National Council for Teachers of Mathematics.

Index